The basics of *Sikhism* is co-authored by two eminent scholars, reflecting their lifelong engagement with the primary and secondary sources. It is a welcome addition to the field of Sikh studies. Written in lucid style, its main appeal is to students and scholars alike, including the general readers. It belongs to the library of every Sikh household settled throughout the world.

– *Pashaura Singh*, **Distinguished Professor and Saini Chair in Sikh Studies, University of California Riverside**

This excellent introduction text to Sikhism is both concise and comprehensive and combines engagement with clarity.

– *Knut A. Jacobsen*, **Professor in the Study of Religions, University of Bergen**

SIKHISM

THE BASICS

Sikhism: The Basics provides an accessible, up-to-date, and gender-inclusive introduction to one of the five major world religions. The chronological and geographic parameters of the book are expansive, tracing five and half centuries – from the vision of the founder Guru (Nanak 1469–1539) to its rich diasporic presence across the globe. *Sikhism: The Basics* includes chapters on

- the ten Sikh Gurus; a historical overview from the post-Guru period to modern times (contextualized by the history of Sikhs' spiritual capital, Amritsar);
- theological imaginary and practices;
- the Sikh diaspora (Sikhs' history in North America, Asia [from West Asia to Southeast Asia and China], Australasia, the United Kingdom, and mainland Europe);
- Sikh art and literature; and
- contemporary challenges and future prospects.

The book is written by two authors approaching *Sikhism* from "insider" (Nikky-Guninder Kaur Singh) and "outsider" (Eleanor Nesbitt) perspectives. It is accessible to the general reader and also offers a fresh approach for students and scholars in the study of religions, Sikh studies, Asian religions, anthropology and diaspora studies, South Asia, and history.

Nikky-Guninder Kaur Singh is Crawford Family Professor and Chair of Religious Studies at Colby College in Maine, USA. She has published extensively in Sikh studies. Her recent books include: *Guru Nanak's Transcendent Aesthetics* (Cambridge University, 2025), *Poems from the Sikh Sacred Tradition* (Harvard University, 2023), *Janamsakhi: Paintings of Guru Nanak in Early Sikh Art* (Roli, 2023), and *The First Sikh: The Life and Legacy of Guru Nanak* (Penguin, 2019).

Eleanor Nesbitt is Professor Emeritus, University of Warwick, UK. Her publications include *Sikhism: A Very Short Introduction, Second Edition* (Oxford University Press, 2016), *Open to New Light: Quakers and Other Faiths* (Collective Ink, 2023), and *Sikh: Two Centuries of Western Women's Art and Writing* (Kashi House, 2024).

The Basics

CHRISTIAN ETHICS
ROBIN GILL

BAHA'I FAITH
CHRISTOPHER BUCK

QUAKERISM
MARGERY POST ABBOTT AND CARL ABBOTT

THOMAS AQUINAS
FRANKLIN T. HARKINS

BIBLE AND FILM
MATTHEW S. RINDGE

RELIGION AND FILM
JEANETTE REEDY SOLANO

SECULARISM
JACQUES BERLINERBLAU

NEW RELIGIOUS MOVEMENTS
JOSEPH LAYCOCK

FILM MUSIC
KENNETH LAMPL

JEWISH ETHICS
GEOFFREY D. CLAUSSEN

QUAKERISM (SECOND EDITION)
MARGERY POST ABBOTT AND CARL ABBOTT

SIKHISM
NIKKY-GUNINDER KAUR SINGH AND ELEANOR NESBITT

For more information about this series, please visit: https://www.routledge.com/The-Basics/book-series/B

SIKHISM

THE BASICS

Nikky-Guninder Kaur Singh and Eleanor Nesbitt

Routledge
Taylor & Francis Group
LONDON AND NEW YORK

Designed cover image: Nora Carol Photography from Getty Images

First published 2025
by Routledge
4 Park Square, Milton Park, Abingdon, Oxon OX14 4RN

and by Routledge
605 Third Avenue, New York, NY 10158

Routledge is an imprint of the Taylor & Francis Group, an informa business

British Library Cataloguing-in-Publication Data
A catalogue record for this book is available from the British Library

Library of Congress Cataloging-in-Publication Data
A catalog record has been requested for this book

ISBN: 978-1-032-41676-2 (hbk)
ISBN: 978-1-032-41677-9 (pbk)
ISBN: 978-1-003-35921-0 (ebk)

DOI: 10.4324/9781003359210

Typeset in Sabon
by Taylor & Francis Books

CONTENTS

List of illustrations xii
Acknowledgments xiii
Authors' Note xiv

1 **Beginnings: The Sikh Gurus** 1

Founder Guru Nanak 2
Biographical Sources 3
Child Rebel 3
Extensive Traveler 4
Visionary Prophet 6
Inspirational Poet 6
Pragmatic Philosopher 8
Historical Gurus: Nanak's Nine Successors 10
Guru Angad (Nanak 2) 1504–1552 11
Guru Amar Das (Nanak 3) 1479–1574 12
Guru Ram Das (Nanak 4) 1534–1581 13
Guru Arjan (Nanak 5) 1563–1606 14
Guru Hargobind (Nanak 6) 1590–1644 15
Guru Har Rai (Nanak 7) 1630–1661 16
Guru Har Krishan (Nanak 8) 1656–1664 17

Guru Tegh Bahadar (Nanak 9) 1621–1675 17
Guru Gobind Singh (Nanak 10) 1666–1708 18
Scriptural Guru: The Guru Granth Sahib 20
Compilation of the Granth 20
Granth Appointed as the Guru 23
Notes 24
References and Further Reading 24

2 A Historical Overview from the Post-Guru Period to Modern Times 25

Introduction 25
Conflict and Conflict Resolution 28
Maharaja Ranjit Singh 32
Sikh-British Interaction 35
Sikh Reform Movements 37
Jallianwala Bagh 39
Regaining Control of Historical Sacred Sites 40
Groupings within the Panth 41
Sikhs in Independent India 41
Code of Discipline 42
A Sikh-Majority State 43
1984 and After 44
Concluding Reflections 45
Notes 46
References and Further Reading 47

3 Theological Imaginary and Existential Reality 48

Theological Matrix: The Mūl Mantar 48
One Being (*Ikkoankār*) 49
Truth Its Name (*Sat Nām*) 51
Creator Person (*Kartā Purakh*) 52
Without Fear (*Nirbhao*) 54
Without Hostility (*Nirvairu*) 56
Timeless Image (*Akāl Murat*) 56
Birthless (*Ajunī*) 56
Self-Existent (*Saibhan*) 57
Gift of the Guru (*Gurprasād*) 57

Theological Intersections: *Hukam, Lekhā, Qudrat, Nadar, Karam*, and *Mukti* 58
Hukam (*Creative Design*) 58
Lekhā (*the Writing*) 60
Qudrat *(Creation, Nature)* 61
Nadar *(Loving Look)* 62
Karam *(Actions)* 62
Mukti *(Freedom)* 64
Theological Quest: The Five Khaṇḍs 65
Ontic: *Dharam* (Morality) 65
Epistemology: *Gīān* (Knowledge) 67
Aesthetic: *Saram* (Beauty) 68
Ethics: *Karam* (Actions) 69
Ultimate Liberation: *Sac* (Truth) 69
Notes 70
References and Further Reading 70

4 Practices **72**

Sikh Sacred Text: The Guru Granth Sahib 72
Sikh Sacred Space: Gurdwara 74
Five Daily Prayers 75
Key Sikh Institutions 77
Sangat 77
Kīrtan 79
Langar 80
Sevā 82
Annual Celebrations 84
Gurpurabs 84
Melās 85
Rites of Passage 86
Name Giving 86
Amrit Initiation 87
Anand Kāraj 88
Death Rites 89
Cultural Festivals 90
Conclusion 92
Notes 93
References and Further Reading 94

5 Sikh Diaspora **96**

Introduction 96
Asia, Australasia, and Africa 100
North America 102
Europe 104
The United Kingdom 104
Mainland Europe 107
Turban and Kirpān *Disputes 108*
Gurdwaras and Religious Socialization 110
Other Diaspora Developments 112
Punjab Politics 112
Media 113
Sport 113
Education 114
Philanthropy 115
Sants 115
Langar and Sevā 116
Literature, Art, and Film 117
Notes 118
References and Further Reading 119

6 Art and Literature **121**

Introduction 121
Scriptural Manuscripts 122
The Janamsākhīs 123
The Ten Gurus 124
Sikh Empire 126
The Golden Temple 127
Western Representations 128
Women Subjects 130
Early Colonial Period 130
Patiala on the Art Map 130
Architect Bhai Ram Singh 131
Later Colonial Period 131
Artists 131
Writers 132
Postcolonial Writing in India 135
Diaspora Sikh Writing and Film 138

Painters 140
Art in Diaspora 142
Notes 144
References and Further Reading 146

7 Contemporary Challenges and Future Prospects 147

Historical Prognoses 147
Farmers' Protest, 2020–2021 148
Religious Realignment and Demography 149
Christianity 150
Derās 151
Sants 152
Calendar Controversy 153
Current Trends and Dilemmas 155
Gender Disparity 155
Sexuality 158
Beadabī 159
Substance Abuse 160
Calls for an Independent Sikh State 160
Revival of Tradition 161
Martial Art 161
Women's Dress 162
Music 162
Kartarpur 163
Conclusion 164
Notes 165
References and Further Reading 166

Glossary 167

Index **172**

ILLUSTRATIONS

3.1 *Ikkoankār*, symbol of unicity 49
5.1 *Khanḍā*, emblem consisting of three swords and a quoit 111

ACKNOWLEDGMENTS

We are grateful to our anonymous readers for their suggestions and to the team at Routledge for their support throughout the publishing process. Our special thanks to Rebecca Clintworth for inspiring us to start the project and to Katie Beaumont for helping us conclude it.

AUTHORS' NOTE

Diacritics have been used for Sikh scriptural verses but not on all the most frequently used Punjabi words. The term "*sac*" is pronounced as the English "such."

1

BEGINNINGS
THE SIKH GURUS

In the present world everything is measured in economic terms and the importance of the most powerful nations is based on their financial strength. Could we have ever imagined that the most powerful economic body of the world i.e. World Bank would be headed by a Guru Sikh?

—Tarlochan Singh, Ex-Member, Parliament of India, and Former Chairman, National Commission for Minorities

In November 2024 the cover of *Time* magazine showed Ajaypal Singh Banga, a turban-wearing Sikh. *Time* listed him as one of the "100 most influential leaders driving business to real climate action." Ajaypal Singh Banga had begun his five-year term as World Bank Group president on June 2, 2023, and Sikhs celebrated it as a day of thanksgiving. The word *Sikh* means "student" or "disciple," and "Guru Sikh" (or, more usually, "Gursikh") means a disciple of the **Guru**. With their spirit of adventure and entrepreneurial skills, Sikhs have migrated from their homeland, Punjab, throughout India and around the globe. There are between 26 million and 30 million Sikhs today, and Sikhs contribute significantly in diverse fields. The defining feature of Sikh ethics – ***sevā*** (to work for the collective good) – was instantly expressed by Mr. Banga in his avowed aim "to create a world free from poverty on a livable planet" (New York City, June 2, 2023). The backdrop of this news item is the development of the Sikh religion over five and a half centuries.

DOI: 10.4324/9781003359210-1

FOUNDER GURU NANAK

Sikh religion began with its founder Guru Nanak although, of course, both his life and the Sikh religion relate in numerous ways to both earlier and contemporary religious insights. The word "Guru" does not refer to any particular god, teacher, text, or an epistemic system as such but is the medium that enables recognition of the same divine One suffused in all beings. The Guru brings forth the awareness of the infinite One that, as Sikhs believe, all individuals have within them, but because of the selfish "I-me" (*haumaï*), most remain oblivious. Starting with Nanak, the ten living Gurus are regarded by Sikhs as illuminators of the divine One, rather than as incarnating the Divine. Guru Nanak's revelation of the One was carried forward by his nine successors and is, Sikhs believe, forever embodied in the Guru Granth Sahib (GGS), the scriptural Guru. The Sikh terms **Waheguru** and **Satguru** (which have often been translated into English as "God") actually designate the singular wondrous (*wāh*) truth (*sat*).

Nanak was born in a Hindu family to mother, Tripta, and father, Kalu, in 1469 in the village of Talvandi (now renamed Nankana Sahib) in pre-partitioned Punjab, in the northwest of the Indian subcontinent. When he was still a teenager, Nanak's marriage was arranged with Sulakhani, and they had two sons. He had a close bond with his sister Nanaki, and as a young adult he lived with her and her husband. In the Sikh collective memory, it was his sister Nanaki who handed the rabāb (a plucked stringed instrument) to his childhood friend Bhai Mardana whose melodious notes subsequently accompanied Guru Nanak's inspirational songs.

Successive invasions and changes of dynasty meant that Punjab's history was layered by the Greeks, Scythians, Sassanids, Huns, Afghans, Persians, Turks, and during his lifetime, the **Mughals**. For centuries the fertile Punjab (or Panjab), land of the five (*panj*) rivers (*āb* = literally water), had been attracting people of different religions and ethnicities. Songs of **Bhagats** and **Sufis**, the lovers of God from a variety of Indic and Islamic traditions, filled the air. ***Bhakti***, a theistic Hindu devotional movement that started in South India in the sixth century, was flourishing in the north by the time of Guru Nanak's birth. Meanwhile, as a result of the Muslim conquest of northern India, charismatic Sufis from Afghanistan and Central Asia had established their orders and sanctified the medieval Indian landscape with Sufi shrines (*dargāhs*), retreats (*khanqāhs*), community kitchens (***langars***), and mosques.

BIOGRAPHICAL SOURCES

We do not have factual documentation, but ***janamsākhīs*** (narratives about Nanak's life) began to circulate orally and were subsequently written down and illustrated. *Janamsākhīs* are, indeed, among the earliest works in the Punjabi language and have generated beautiful paintings as well as an abundant literary repertoire. They depict the first Sikh Guru's interior and exterior journeys, his interfaith conversations, and his actions. Their condensed prose incorporating poetic excerpts, all written in **Gurmukhi** script, has enormous vernacular appeal. Quasi-mythically they weave the Sikh Guru's imagined biography from his poetry. Their settings, protagonists, scriptural citations, drama, magic, and moral message flesh out his philosophical vision and ethical teachings. For generations Sikh parents and grandparents have read the *janamsākhīs* as bedtime stories, so nurturing their children with different levels of meaning for the rest of their lives. The poetic works of Bhai Gurdas, the earliest Sikh theologian (1551–1636), corroborate the *janamsākhī* narratives by illuminating the person and role of Guru Nanak. The various sources unanimously depict Guru Nanak's rebellious impulse, his extensive travels, his divine revelation, his poetic expertise, his pluralistic worldview, and his kindling of a new religiosity.

CHILD REBEL

The *janamsākhīs* suggest, retrospectively, a spiritually oriented youngster discontented with society's prescribed norms. For example, on his first day at school they portray him rejecting the customary instruction; instead, he questions and ends up teaching the teacher to write with a pen of love on a clean mind without any prejudices. Later, they suggest, he disrupted his initiation (*upanyāna*), the important thread (*janeu*) ceremony reserved for upper-caste boys. According to Sikh tradition, during this crucial rite of passage that had upheld the hierarchical and exclusivist **caste** system, Nanak refused to wear the sacred cotton thread, demanding instead a thread made of compassion and spun with truth. Likewise, when his father gave him money to start a business, he went to the hungry ascetics and spent his money feeding them. There are many such traditional narratives, all based on literal interpretations of the imagery and metaphor of his own poetry, that illustrate Nanak's revolutionary impulse. By interrogating his teacher he sought to break customary intellectual habits and doctrines; by refusing to wear the sacred thread, he tried to dismantle societal hegemonies of caste and class; by feeding the ascetics, he challenged their ideal of worldly renunciation and the conventional fear of the body.

Indeed, contemporary society hinged on the binary of the sacred and the secular, a binary that he must have battled existentially. His peers were the Siddhs, Yogis, Sufi saints, Hindu *bhagat*s, Buddhist monks, and Jain renunciates, who practiced holiness by avoiding marriage and household ties. Women were considered obstacles to men's progress on the spiritual path. The narratives relay Nanak's emphasis on love and a joyous mode of existence.

EXTENSIVE TRAVELER

According to tradition, Nanak initially left his wife and sons and, with his Muslim companion Bhai Mardana, traveled extensively. The *janamsākhī*s repeatedly portray Guru Nanak – with wit and irony – denouncing formal ritual. For instance, during his travels, when visiting Hardwar, the ancient site of pilgrimage on the river Ganges, Nanak saw some brahmins offering water to the rising sun in the east, and he instead started tossing water to the west. The brahmins found his actions sacrilegious. When they asked him who would benefit from casting water to the west, he posed them a similar question. The priests responded that they were offering oblations to appease the spirits of dead ancestors. Nanak then continued his procedure even more vigorously, thus making the point that if the brahmins' water could reach dead ancestors, surely his would irrigate his own fields in nearby Punjab – in other words, their ritual actions were futile.

This pedagogical pattern recurs in the *janamsākhī* narratives, with Nanak overturning the established ritual codes in a way that challenges assumptions and orients people toward a new reality. While the numerous miracles attributed to him probably originated in his followers' reverence for him, they can also serve hearers and readers today as lenses for interrogating the inner workings of their own mind. For example, when Guru Nanak went to Mecca, he reputedly fell asleep with his feet toward the Ka'ba. When the officiating *qāzī* protested at the visitor's irreverence, Guru Nanak politely asked him to turn his feet toward somewhere that God was absent. But as his feet were turned, the sacred Ka'ba also revolved. Of course, this is not a historical fact but makes a clear point about the ubiquitous divine presence and also collapses the brahmins' hegemony of the "thinking head" over the "defiling feet." In this way, simple narratives can dislocate conventional habits and structures.

During his long travels Guru Nanak must have visited Hindu temples, Muslim mosques, Buddhist *vihārā*s, and Sufi *khanqāh*s, and he probably attended many fairs and festivals. Wherever he went he engaged the local inhabitants in discussion and dialogue. For instance, in one scenario, he climbed up a mountain to meet a group of venerable holy men. Their shaved heads, lengthened ear lobes (their name "*kan-phat*" meaning "ear split"), their long earrings and ash-smeared bodies indicated their arduous yoga practices and ascetic ideals. Guru Nanak put to them the sanctity of the body and urged them to shoulder the responsibilities of normal social life.

Traveling on foot, he no doubt acquired an appreciative knowledge of the abundant diversity of plants, trees, birds, landscapes, and climate, as well as people's diverse beliefs, sacred places, practices, and languages. He would have absorbed diversity – environmental, cultural, linguistic, and religious.

VISIONARY PROPHET

The spiritual seeker discovered a new way of being in the world that would subsequently give rise to the Sikh religion. He had a prophetic vision of the infinite ***ikkoankār***, the One encompassing all beings and things. He experienced the infinite unity viscerally and therefore needed no ontological, epistemological, teleological, or moral arguments to prove its existence. Importantly, he gave the One the name of truth (***sat nām***) so that people could actively engage with it. Nanak's One does not hold on to any existing form of god or goddess or claim inheritance from any Hindu, Islamic, Buddhist, or Jain precept, although "*oan*" (*om*) is the primal vocalic syllable of the Indian languages.

Nanak experienced unicity (oneness) here and now, in and through the body. The five senses (*giān indriā*) – tasting, hearing, smelling, touching, and seeing – were integral to his metaphysical thought and his existential praxis. They can either be honed into the five virtues of truth (*sat*), contentment (*santokh*), morality (***dharam***), compassion (*daiā*), and tenacity (*dhīraj*), or conversely, they can degenerate into five vices: lust (*kām*), anger (*krodh*), greed (*lobh*), attachment (*moh*), and pride (*ahankār*). They encode Guru Nanak's moral compass: the *gurmukh*s oriented toward the infinite One, and *manmukh*s who face their egoistic self. How anybody understands the One, and how they enact in their daily affairs a sense of that One, is contingent on their bodily sensibilities. Whereas many lovers of God (religious devotees) and lovers of knowledge (philosophers) disparage bodily associations, for Guru Nanak the five were instrumental for the experience of divine unity and its reflex reactions in daily life. Accordingly, chapter 3 is built on his theological imaginary and these ethical paradigms.

INSPIRATIONAL POET

From his experience of unicity poured out poetry full of passion and compassion. Guru Nanak's corpus of 974 compositions, the nub of Sikh philosophy, ethics, and aesthetics, was recorded in Sikh scripture, the Guru Granth Sahib, by his successor Gurus. His entire oeuvre hymns the glorious One, the matrix of space and time. His **Japji** composition (the opening of the Guru Granth Sahib) embraces countless musicians, instruments, melodies, and wide-ranging voices. It evokes a unison of gods, sages, beautiful women, water, wind, fire, heroes, ascetics, jewels, species, continents, constellations, and universes. Peacocks, frogs, songbirds, serpents, fish, sparrows, ants, and deer all feature in his literary and musical repertoire.

Imbued with his love for the singular Divine, Guru Nanak's verse prescribes no rules, gives no doctrinal or epistemic system to follow; instead, the lyrics motivate listeners and readers to search for themselves, think about their choices, and to act for the collective good. Poetically Guru Nanak challenges and overturns assumptions and stretches the imagination.

Guru Nanak's poetry appears in a variety of genres including metaphysical compositions, acrostics, songs of mourning, ballads, philosophical discourses, and several compositions on the theme of time. The timeless One is "true in the beginning, true across the ages, true now also, Nanak: true for ever more" (GGS: 1). Many of Guru Nanak's poems convey his fascination with time, drawing attention to temporality and the role and responsibility of humans passing through time. He innovatively utilized the poetic genres of North Indian devotional poets – genres such as "The Hours," "Days of the Lunar Month," and "Song of the Twelve Months." His poetry appears in different meters, rhymes, stanzas, and compositional styles. Its building blocks are essentially short half verses of three of four words. These brief units sequentially take on the form of two-stanza compositions (*dupade*), four stanzas (*caupade*), eight stanzas (*ashtpade*), four stanzas of six verses (*chhant*), and even sixteen-stanza compositions (*solahe*), and many of them go on to form the longer *vārs* (ballads). His compositions, intersecting as they do with historical moments (during the Mughal Babur's invasion of North India, in particular), are relevant to future generations' cultural, political, psychological, social, spiritual, and environmental needs.

Guru Nanak's "language of infinite love" (*bhākhiā bhāo apāru* [GGS: 2]) enables readers to recollect the infinite One. The sense of plenitude strips off patriarchal stratifications. Thus, one short composition portrays the Divine as the bride in her wedding dress and also as the groom on the nuptial bed . . . as the fisherman, the fish, the waters, the trap, the weight holding the net, as well as the lost ruby swallowed by the fish! Male and female are balanced in his theological imaginary. It is also noteworthy that nothing in the cosmos is deemed too low for the divine to sparkle through. Humans are not the only ones endowed with spiritual treasures. Guru Nanak's literary tropes parallel natural phenomena.

Moreover, he expresses his spiritual longing with a feminine consciousness. Frequently he adopts women's tone, mood, activities, and accoutrements to voice his spiritual desire. He even identifies with females of several species: a doe living in the jungles, a koel singing in the mango grove, a fish dwelling in the waters, and a she-serpent in a hole. He hears the sparrow calling for God in Persian (*khudāi khudāi*). Guru Nanak's linguistic and imaginative fusion endows the female with a transcendent value. Arguably, the animal world is not used allegorically to represent the affairs of the human world: rather, the two worlds are essentially one and the same. Poet Nanak overcomes male-female, human-animal divides, expanding subjectivity across genders and species.

PRAGMATIC PHILOSOPHER

The prophet poet was also a pragmatic philosopher envisioning social reform. Guru Nanak sought to build an infrastructure for his divine revelation to have real-world consequences. On concluding his travels, on the banks of the river Ravi, he started the Kartarpur community which was subsequently to develop into a town. In this first Sikh community there were, Sikhs believe, no divisions between sacred and secular. Monastic practices were rejected; spiritual life amid marriage, family, and community was valued. Men and women from different religious and social backgrounds came to hear and recite divine praise and to practice equality and inclusivity. Together they grew crops, harvested, and prepared and ate meals. Their routine of reciting Nanak's Japji in the morning and Sodar and Arati in the evening is still repeated in Sikh homes and places of worship. The practices of ***sangat*** (coming together) of *sevā* (working selflessly), *langar* (cooking and eating collectively), and ***kīrtan*** (exalting the infinite One) were further developed by Guru Nanak's successors as key Sikh institutions (see chapter 4).

Theoretically this new way of "Sikh" life birthed by Guru Nanak in Kartarpur is what cultural anthropologist Victor Turner calls "antistructure." It was an existential revolt against the ancient fourfold class structure with its rigid hierarchical codes and male-female gender divisions. No body, whether Shudra/**Dalit** or female, was polluted. Guru Nanak categorically stated that pollution did not reside in any person or object; pollution was an artificial mental construction imposed by the privileged.

Rather than using the Devanagari or Arabic scripts of the more highbrow Sanskrit or Persian, Guru Nanak probably used Gurmukhi (although it is the second Guru who is more often accredited with developing this script). The characters resemble the *laṇḍḍe/mahājanī* business shorthand of his hereditary commercial community that he himself would have probably used during his apprenticeship in storehouses. The Gurmukhi script (literally "from the Guru's mouth") is introduced in his acrostic "Paṭī Likhī" (Writing on the Board, GGS: 432–434). Alphabet acrostics for Arabic and Devanagari scripts were popular in his milieu, and most of the stanzas of Guru Nanak's acrostic begin with letters of Gurmukhi. Like the Bhagats and many Sufis, he composed in the local vernacular, so releasing religious language from the custody of the authorities of his day.

Before his death Guru Nanak appointed his disciple Lahina as his successor. By selecting him rather than either of his two sons, he decisively broke away from patrilineal structure: he gave Lahina his book of verse and named him Angad. Guru Nanak's contemporaries would have recalled Angad, a key helper of Rama and Sita in the Ramayana, and *aṅgad* means an ornament too, but Sikhs understand Lahina's new name to mean that he was the Guru's very own limb (*aṅg*). Indeed, a bodily link with poetry is underscored in several stories about Guru Nanak. In one he is bathing with a jug of water, watched by his future successor, Guru Angad. Pointing to a blue-black patch of skin on his ribcage, Guru Nanak explains to Angad that the night before, a young shepherd had been reciting his hymns on ground covered with thorny bushes, and Guru Nanak was accidentally scratched brushing against them. This narrative strikingly conveys his physical presence in his verse. A memorable late 19th-century illustration shows Guru Nanak wearing an outfit with verses from the Guru Granth Sahib and the holy Qur'an inscribed all over his front and sleeve (Government Museum and Art Gallery in Chandigarh). In this way, the Guru is shown effacing divisions between himself (*gurū*) and his poetry (*bāṇī*), between Sikh and Muslim, body and spirit, language and reality, the temporal and the timeless. Poetry was his medium for awakening his contemporaries – unlike Plato who banned the poets from his republic because "poetry feeds and waters the passions instead of drying them up," Guru Nanak used poetry to drench his parched society with his vision of the One.

Paradoxically, though, Guru Nanak with his experience of the borderless divine and his inclusive praxis succeeded in creating a distinct tradition – one that is remarkably vibrant the world over five centuries later. The over 26 million Sikhs have their particular sacred text (Guru Granth Sahib), their sacred space (**gurdwara**), their physical identity (5 Ks – see below), and their socioreligious institutions. Foundational to this was Guru Nanak's revelatory experience, soon after which he is believed to have said, "There is no Hindu, there is no Muslim." The statement can be interpreted as a critique of institutionalized religions. Arguably, what today's divided society needs is Guru Nanak's transreligiosity, transcending as it does such categories as monotheism, polytheism, and atheism.

HISTORICAL GURUS: NANAK'S NINE SUCCESSORS

Guru Nanak's nine successors, the Gurus from Guru Angad (1504–1552) to Guru Gobind Singh (1666–1708), carried on his spiritual legacy. The content of their instruction was the same, as also was the poetic method they utilized. Indeed, Sikhs believe that they personified the same light and that the same voice spoke through all ten. The transference of guruship was repeated successively until the tenth ended the line of personal Gurus in 1708 by investing the role of Guru in the scripture, the poetic anthology compiled by the fifth Guru in 1604 to which the ninth Guru's compositions had by then been added. The lives of the ten Gurus are poetically recollected in Sarup Das Bhalla's *Mahima Prakash* (1776) and Santokh Singh's *Suraj Prakash Granth* (1843).[1]

Guru Nanak (1469–1539)
Guru Angad (1504–1552)
Guru Amar Das (1479–1574)
Guru Ram Das (1534–1581)
Guru Arjan (1563–1606)
Guru Hargobind (1590–1644)
Guru Har Rai (1630–1661)
Guru Har Krishan (1656–1664)
Guru Tegh Bahadar (1621–1675)
Guru Gobind Singh (1666–1708)

GURU ANGAD (NANAK 2) 1504–1552

Upon his succession, Guru Angad helped the nascent community grow and spread for 13 years. Like Nanak, he valued poetry's aesthetic and epistemological power. He developed and standardized the Gurmukhi script and composed 62 couplets. To signal the spiritual and poetic continuity, he signed them "Nanak" and added them to Guru Nanak's compositions. The first Guru's ideals and diction echo in Guru Angad's verse. He evoked the ever present singular one (*ek/ikk*) in the fluctuating course of the day and across the spheres, urging audiences to discover the wealth of nine great treasures (*navanidh*) within this body (*sarīr*) (GGS: 46). Metaphorically he related with the infinite One as a goldsmith or jeweler, adding luster to the golden bodies doing good deeds (GGS: 146). He also satirically critiqued prevailing norms and practices.

After carrying on the office of Guru Nanak in Kartarpur, the second Guru moved to the village of Khadur, strengthening the institutions of *sangat, sevā, kīrtan,* and *langar*. His wife, Mata Khivi, is extolled for her cooking skills and liberal distribution of the *langar* meal. (Mata, meaning "mother" is a respectful title.) In the words of the bard Balvand in the Guru Granth Sahib:

> Says Balvand, Khivi is a noble person, a leafy shade.
> She abundantly dispenses langar, her rice pudding drenched in ghee tastes ambrosial.
>
> GGS: 967

Like a shady tree, Mata Khivi provides comfort to all. The *khīr* she prepares – a dish made of rice, milk, and sugar – has the immortal quality of ***amrit***.

Their daughter Bibi Amro ("Bibi" too being a respectful title) played an important role in the continuation of Guru Nanak's spiritual legacy because it was from her lips that Amar Das (Bibi Amro's husband's uncle) overheard Guru Nanak's verse. When Amar Das expressed his wish to meet the Guru, Bibi Amro escorted Amar Das to her father, Guru Angad, in her natal village. Although Amar Das was much older, he became a devoted follower of the second Guru and later succeeded him as Guru.

GURU AMAR DAS (NANAK 3) 1479–1574

The third Guru established the town of Goindval for the solidification and expansion of the community. To reach distant congregations, he set up 22 seats of authority. Pious Sikh men and women were appointed leaders. They taught Guru Nanak's message, looked after the congregation in their jurisdiction, and transmitted the disciples' offerings to Goindval. During the traditional spring and autumn festivals of Baisakhi and Divālī, the congregations were encouraged to visit Goindval, thus fostering a sense of their own "Sikh" celebrations. Guru Amar Das had built a large well with 84 steps in Goindval to provide drinking water, and for the Sikhs it began to serve as a special meeting place.

Guru Amar Das's daughter was Bibi Bhani, the wife of the future fourth Guru and the mother of the fifth. She must have influenced Guru Amar Das who was attentive to the oppressed condition of women. He denounced women's segregation and appointed them as leaders. Guru Amar Das invokes gender equality in the verse, "Do not call them husband and wife who merely sit side by side; husband and wife are two bodies who share the same light" (GGS: 788), so calling for effective equality, an authentic union empowering both men and women, socially and spiritually.

With Guru Amar Das there is actual evidence of the scriptural text in the making. Two volumes of poetry in the Gurmukhi script by his predecessors and some saints were created under his supervision in the town of Goindval. He too composed fine poetry. All Sikh rites and ceremonies conclude with the congregation reciting together sections of his composition "Anand" (meaning "bliss"), which has also been incorporated into the evening prayer. Anand opens with, "My Mother! I am in bliss, for I have found my true Guru; my true Guru I found so easily, my mind rings with felicitations." The readers enter with the Guru a sphere with no divisions or defense mechanisms. There are 907 such lyrical hymns of Guru Amar Das included in the Guru Granth Sahib. Before he passed away, he chose Bibi Bhani's husband, Ram Das, as his successor.

GURU RAM DAS (NANAK 4) 1534–1581

The fourth Guru too composed sacred poetry and fostered the self-consciousness of the community. His composition "Lāvān" now serves as the basis for the Sikh wedding ceremony. *Lāvān* (circling) describes marriage as a rite of passage into deeper and deeper circles of existence. The journey begins with active engagement in society and divine adoration. The second verse describes the realization of the singular One within all that is seen and heard. In the third circle, that feeling surges, and the self becomes fully absorbed in divine love. As the fourth round commences, elixir begins to pervade the entire self, uniting the individual with the all-pervasive One. Marriage is thus both literal and metaphorical: literally it is a union of two people and metaphorically a union of the finite person with the infinite One. Husband and wife begin a fulfilling sensual-spiritual life together.

The fourth Guru is notably remembered for the founding of Amritsar, which, as we shall see in chapter 2, continues to feature importantly in the development of the Sikh religion. The town was originally called Ramdaspur after him, and since it was located near the Delhi-Kabul trade route, it prospered. It soon became the focal point for Sikhs to gather during spring and autumn festivals, and during the guruship of his son and successor, Guru Arjan, Amritsar became the religious capital of the Sikhs. Importantly, the fourth Guru's verse "*hori manmukh dāj ji rakh dikhāleh su kūṛ ahankār kac pājo*" (GGS: 78–79) uses the Punjabi word *dāj* for "egocentric showing off, a false arrogant, flimsy display" and is understood as a prohibition of dowry – a practice that continues to be a blatant commodification of daughters that creates a terrible burden and humiliation for parents. During the time of the fourth Guru, Dalits from the Julaha (weaver) caste looking for human dignity and social equality converted to Sikhism.[2]

GURU ARJAN (NANAK 5) 1563–1606

The first 11 years of Guru Arjan's life were spent at Goindval with his parents, Bibi Bhani and Guru Ram Das, in the home of his maternal grandfather, Guru Amar Das. In this town, located on the imperial highway between Delhi and Lahore, young Arjan learned Gurmukhi, Sanskrit, and Persian. As noted by the Sikh studies scholar Pashaura Singh, Guru Arjan received training in classical rāgas from both resident and visiting musicians in Ramdaspur and Lahore. He married Ganga Devi and spent time in Lahore where he set up the morning and evening patterns of Sikh worship. He would have made the most of the vibrant atmosphere of Lahore by visiting Sufi centers and interacting with people of different faiths. In 1581 Guru Ram Das chose Arjan to succeed him as the fifth Guru, and this antagonized Guru Arjan's eldest brother.

Thanks to Guru Arjan, the Sikh religion acquired strong scriptural, doctrinal, and organizational foundations. Sikh philanthropy and social commitment expanded beyond the welfare of the community. Guru Arjan initiated new construction projects in Ramdaspur and completed the excavation of sacred pools of Amritsar, Santokhsar, and Ramsar started by his father. When a famine hit Punjab, he traveled from village to village, helping people sink wells and undertake several other works for public welfare. As a result, many more people were brought into the Sikh fold. He also established new Sikh centers and laid the foundation for the new town of Tarn Taran.

Guru Arjan's historical and political backdrop was the Mughal empire. Emperor Akbar with his liberal religious vision brought people together for interreligious discussions and produced a new "Divine Faith" (*Dīn-i-Ilāhī*). As noted by historians, Akbar also visited Guru Arjan. Interestingly, just when Persian was becoming the lingua franca of the Mughal administration, Guru Arjan compiled the sacred **Granth**, which (despite its linguistic diversity) has come to be regarded as the first anthology in the Punjabi language. He himself composed over 2,000 superb **shabads** (devotional verses, hymns). He constructed the **Harmandar**, which would subsequently become the Golden Temple, and enshrined in it the sacred volume. The Guru articulated a Sikh identity distinct from both Hindu and Muslim traditions:

> I do not make the Hajj nor any Hindu pilgrimage, I serve the One and no other. I neither perform Hindu worship nor do I offer Muslim prayers, I have taken the formless One into my heart. I am neither Hindu nor Muslim.
>
> (GGS: 1136)

However, after Emperor Akbar's death, the political climate changed, and the fifth Guru was tortured to death. Sources offer various reasons for this. His martyrdom generated resistance and inaugurated for his followers a new era of martial élan. Guru Arjan's compilation of the Guru Granth Sahib and his building of the Harmandar proved to be vital in strengthening Sikh psyche and Sikh identity.

GURU HARGOBIND (NANAK 6) 1590–1644

Guru Hargobind, the sixth Guru, was the only son of Guru Arjan and Mata Ganga. He was educated in religious texts and trained in swordsmanship and archery and was barely 11 years old when he lost his father. According to Sikh tradition, for his succession ceremonies the sixth Guru wore a warrior's equipment, along with the rosary and other saintly emblems. He put on two swords – one he called the sword of ***pīrī*** and the other the sword of ***mīrī***. Both of these terms had entered into India with Islam: "*pīrī*," from *pīr* (a religious teacher); "*mīrī*," from *amīr* (a commander of the faithful). The sixth Guru's investment with spiritual and secular authority marked an important development in the evolution of the Sikh community.

Guru Hargobind raised a band of armed Sikhs, and he sent out messages that disciples in the future must come with gifts of horses and weapons. He introduced two martial symbols: the kettledrum and the pennant. The booming kettledrum that was then used to build up his men's heroism is today heard in some gurdwaras in India during the recitation of the ***ardās*** prayer. Likewise, the flag hoisted as a mark (***nishān***) of Sikh sites is also traced back to Guru Hargobind Singh's political sensibility. To defend the town of Amritsar, he built in 1609 a fortress called Loh Garh (Iron Fort). Moreover, as a seat of temporal authority, he had the platform laid for the **Akāl Takht** (Throne of the Timeless One), directly facing the Harmandar. The warrior Guru sat here regally and conducted the secular affairs of his community. Sikh art depicts him as delicate in manner but large and muscular in physique. He has been credited too with creating the beautiful peacock-shaped stringed instrument, the *taus*. He traveled widely in the Punjab and beyond to places like Srinagar in Kashmir spreading the word of Guru Nanak. He had five sons and only one daughter, Bibi Viro.

GURU HAR RAI (NANAK 7) 1630–1661

Guru Hargobind appointed his grandson Har Rai as his successor. The tender sensitivity of the seventh Guru is portrayed in Sikh iconography. In an early 19th-century painting from the family workshop of the famous Nainsukh of Guler, we see the Guru dressed in a translucent white muslin knee-length cloak that matches the delicate white blossoms on the tree across from him. He is on a walk with an attendant carrying a majestic umbrella; the Guru's simple halo symbolizes his inner radiance. Instead of hunting dogs, there is a dog ahead of him, turning back as though to have a peek at the Guru. The imagined scene conveys his spirituality while engaged in his normal routine. The Guru continued to maintain his grandfather's large army of Sikh warriors and he kept alive the military spirit. He is remembered for providing herbal remedies and for protecting animals. He was married and had two sons.

GURU HAR KRISHAN (NANAK 8) 1656–1664

Guru Har Rai appointed his younger son Har Krishan as his successor. The eighth Guru took up leadership of the community at the age of five, but he contracted smallpox and died when he was only eight years old. Bangla Sahib, the central Sikh shrine in Delhi, commemorates the spot where the young Guru had a pool of fresh water dug. As a popular saying goes, “By remembering Sri Har Krishan, all sufferings disperse.” In a cryptic utterance he identified his successor, his great-uncle Tegh Bahadar, the youngest son of Guru Hargobind and Mata Nanaki.

GURU TEGH BAHADAR (NANAK 9) 1621–1675

Guru Tegh Bahadar challenged the policy of the Mughal ruler of converting Hindus by force. According to Sikh tradition (though this is very differently regarded in Mughal records), it was for his defense of religious freedom that he was executed in public in Chandni Chowk, near the Red Fort in Delhi on 11th November 1675.

Guru Tegh Bahadar’s poignant poetry comprising 59 hymns and 56 couplets was added to the Guru Granth Sahib by his son and successor. Like his predecessors, he praised people who enshrine the Divine within because “there is no difference between them and the Divine” (GGS: 43). He defined liberation as a life of equanimity: “For whom praise is the same as blame, and gold is the same as iron, says Nanak, know that person is free” (GGS: 1427). The ninth Guru used numerous innovative similes: “Like fragrance in flower, like reflection in a mirror, the One dwells equally in all” (GGS: 684). His comparisons with other animal species are equally striking: “Worship the Divine single-mindedly, just like a faithful dog” (GGS: 45), but “when there is pride in the heart, pilgrimages, fasts, charities, and other acts are as futile as an elephant’s bath” (GGS: 46). All ceremonial readings of the Guru Granth Sahib conclude with his haunting compositions.

GURU GOBIND SINGH (NANAK 10) 1666–1708

The tenth Guru was born in Patna where his parents, Guru Tegh Bahadar and Mata Gujari, had been living for some time. When he was seven, the family moved to Anandpur, founded by the ninth Guru. Literally "the city of bliss," Anandpur is in the Shivalik foothills. The Mughal empire was at its zenith under Emperor Aurangzeb (1658–1707). Unlike his great-grandfather Akbar, who had abolished the *jizyā* (tax on non-Muslims) and promoted interreligious discussions, and unlike his brother Dara Shikoh who sponsored the translation of several Upanishads into Persian, Aurangzeb tried to make India an exclusively Muslim country. All those who did not practice Islam, including Guru Gobind Singh and his Sikh community, became victims of Aurangzeb's orthodoxy. Deriving sustenance from his mother, Gujari, Guru Gobind Singh quickly transformed the devastating impact of his father's execution into creativity and action: the Divine was remembered, heroic poetry was recited, music was performed, and mock battles took place. Such activities arguably diverted the Sikhs from thoughts of retaliation. Anandpur began to resound with holy hymns and heroic ballads, the galloping of horses, martial exercises, a variety of sports, and with the beating of Guru Gobind Singh's drum of victory. But the neighboring hill kingdoms were threatened by these symbols of political power and so the Guru and his followers ended up fighting several battles.

Like his predecessors, Guru Gobind Singh was a superb poet. Through his poetry he expressed the themes of love, equality, and an ethical and moral code of conduct. Deprecating idolatry and superstitious beliefs and practices, he evoked the singular One. Indeed, when India was bleeding from the wounds of partition in 1947, M.K. Gandhi encouraged peace and harmony with his popular prayer "Ishvara and Allah are your names, temple and mosque are your homes," which evoked Guru Gobind Singh's verses from the Akāl Ustati: "Hindus and Muslims are one. . . . The Hindu temple and the Muslim mosque are the same. . . . All humanity is one" (verse 86).

Guru Gobind Singh's inauguration of the **Khalsa** is deeply etched in the Sikh psyche. The word *khalsa*, meaning "pure," also implies owing no allegiance to subsidiary powers. The visible identity of the Sikhs is generally traced to Baisakhi day 1699, when the Guru initiated five volunteers who were prepared to give up their life for him. Calling them his Five Beloved (*panj pyāre*), the Guru gave them the ambrosial drink (*amrit*) he had prepared by stirring water in a bowl of iron with his double-edged sword (*khanḍā*) while chanting sacred verses. His wife, Mata Jitoji, added sugar puffs, and thus sweetness through the feminine hand mingled with what was widely believed in Punjab to be the alchemy of iron.[3] This event marked Guru Gobind Singh's new fellowship, which would be strong and courageous in resisting any form of tyranny and oppression.

The Five Beloved had come to Anandpur from different parts of India and they belonged to different social classes, but the sipping of *amrit* from the same bowl marked their new relationship with no more social or religious differences. With each sip, ancient norms upholding caste and creed divisions were washed out. Their drinking together defined their new birth and equal membership in the family of the Khalsa. Just as sharing a mother's milk bonds her offspring into a family, so sipping the Guru's *amrit* bonded the Five Beloved into the Khalsa family forever. The five receiving the *amrit* from Guru Gobind Singh were also given the surname of Singh, meaning "lion."

According to tradition, whereas men received the surname Singh, women received from the Guru the surname Kaur (literally "prince" rather than the more usual translation as "princess"), and this became the norm during a period of reform in the 19th century. Certainly, according to Sikh religious teaching (even if not always in practice) both men and women became equal partners in the new Khalsa family. In principle, initiation into the Khalsa means a rebirth into the new egalitarian family – an annihilation of previous family ties, hereditary occupations, beliefs, and rituals. To have faith in the singular Divine and to regard all human beings as equal is the Khalsa mandate.

Single or married (and whether initiated or not), Sikh women today generally retain the second name Kaur. Indeed, it is customary for Sikhs to receive the names Singh and Kaur as infants and many Sikhs do in fact still use their family name as a third name or surname.

According to Sikh tradition, initiated Khalsa Sikhs were also to wear emblems of the Khalsa, which are now popularly known as the **Five Ks**. As further detailed in chapter 4, these are ***kesh*** or long hair and beard; ***kanghā***, a comb tucked into the ***kesh*** to keep it tidy in contrast with the recluses who kept it matted as a token of their having renounced the world; ***kaṛā***, a steel bracelet; ***kacchā***, short breeches worn by the soldiers of Guru Gobind Singh's time; and ***kirpān***, a sword.

Guru Gobind Singh was married to Mata Jito in 1677 and to Mata Sundari in 1684 and had four sons with them: Ajit Singh, Jujhar Singh, Jorawar Singh, and Fateh Singh. His nuptials with Mata Sahib Devan took place in Anandpur in 1700. Eight years later the Guru was assassinated in Nanded, Maharashtra. Shortly before Guru Gobind Singh had ended the human line of succession by investing the scripture with the role of Guru, the Guru Granth Sahib.

SCRIPTURAL GURU: THE GURU GRANTH SAHIB

For Sikhs the scriptural text is the living Guru, the sovereign who presides at all their public and private ceremonies, rites of passage, and worship. Indeed, in 2000, the Supreme Court of India declared the Guru Granth Sahib to have the status of a juristic person.

COMPILATION OF THE GRANTH

The fifth Guru, Guru Arjan, finished compiling the Guru Granth Sahib in 1604, a task that required sustained labor as well as rigorous intellectual discipline. He had spent the first 11 years of his life with his parents in the home of his maternal grandfather where the two Goindval collections had been compiled. Naturally Guru Arjan would have absorbed the inclusivity and precision involved in the textual compilations. The fellowship of Sikhs from the Kartarpur days of Guru Nanak had increased numerically and spread geographically, so there was a need for a central canon for their spiritual and moral life.

With literary finesse, Guru Arjan carried out the work of compiler and editor, and he called on Bhai Gurdas to assist him

(*Bhāī* – literally "brother" – is a term denoting respect for a man). Guru Nanak's pluralism served as the template. Selections were made from the works of the first four Gurus, from Guru Arjan's own expansive repertoire, and from the compositions of Hindu and Muslim saints that were a part of his broader South Asian heritage. Consistently with Guru Nanak, the fifth Guru's approach to external differences in accents, intonations, grammar, vocabulary, or imagery was inclusive. He recorded the spiritual lyrics spanning North India over half a millennium, the earliest being Sheikh Farid's, and delivered a unique text embracing both Islamic monotheistic and Indic polyvalent currents. He brought together a wide range of authors from different regions, centuries, and languages, and Bhai Gurdas recorded them uniformly in the Gurmukhi script. This is not a hybrid assemblage of Hindu-Muslim ideas; the autonomous voices of the various authors with their distinct religious perspectives are retained and validated. Each author is authentically identified.

A list of names of the contributors and numbers of their hymns follows:

Guru Nanak: 974 hymns
Guru Angad: 62 couplets
Guru Amar Das: 907 hymns
Guru Ram Das: 679 hymns
Guru Arjan: 2218 hymns
Guru Tegh Bahadar, the ninth Guru: 59 hymns and 56 couplets
(These were added by his son, Guru Gobind Singh, the tenth Guru.)
Bhagats and Sufis:
Kabir: 292 hymns
Farid: 4 hymns and 130 couplets
Namdev: 60 hymns
Ravidas: 41 hymns
Jaidev: 2 hymns
Beni: 3 hymns
Trilochan: 4 hymns
Parmananda: 1 hymn
Sadhana: 1 hymn
Ramananda: 1 hymn
Dhanna: 4 hymns

Pipa: 1 hymn
Sain: 1 hymn
Bhikhan: 2 hymns
Sur Das: 2 hymns
Sundar: 1 hymn
Mardana: 3 couplets
Satta and Balvand: 1 hymn
Bhatts: 123 *swayyai* (verses praising the Gurus)

The compositions were further arranged into 31 rāga sections. *Rāga* means both "color" and "musical mode" in Sanskrit, and each rāga has a season prescribed for its singing, plus a prescribed time of the day, an emotional mood, and a particular cultural climate as each measure evolved in a specific region. In the Guru Granth Sahib the 31 rāgas appear in a specific order: Sri Rāga, Majh, Gauri, Asa, Gujri, Devgandhari, Bihagara, Wadahans, Sorath, Dhanasri, Jaitsri, Todi, Bairari, Tilang, Suhi, Bilaval, Gaund, Ramkali, Nut-Narayan, Mali-Gaura, Maru, Tukhari, Kedara, Bhairo, Basant, Sarang, Malar, Kanra, Kalyan, Prabhati, and Jaijawanti. The Guru Granth Sahib's spectrum of rāgas welcomes people from diverse cultures, regions, religions, and social backgrounds. Besides classical rāgas, the Guru Granth Sahib includes folk musical patterns with simpler beats, as well as regional Bhakti and Sufi forms with their rhythms and melodies, and wedding songs and mourning lamentations. The Guru Granth Sahib does not subscribe to classical and folk/popular dualisms. Its melodic framework allows a great deal of latitude for improvisation. Transcending verbal systems, music has a communal value that brings people together who may speak different languages.

Each rāga section of the Guru Granth Sahib is structured systematically according to the length and author of the composition. First come the hymns in four stanzas, then hymns in eight stanzas, then those in four stanzas of six verses, which are followed by longer compositions like the ballads (*vārs*). These compositions are further arranged by authorship: they start with the Gurus in order of succession and are followed by the Bhagats and Sufis in the same organizational pattern. Although the Sikh Guru-authors signed their compositions with the name of

Nanak, to show that they were continuing his work, each is clearly identified by the numeral attached to the word *mahallā*. It is Mahallā 1 if the composition belonged to the first Guru, Mahallā 2 if it was by the second Guru, and so on. The word *mahallā* means "ward" or "body," so underscoring that, in Sikh belief, the Gurus are a corporeal and spiritual continuity.

Since it records the voice of some of the founding fathers of the Indian religious traditions, the Guru Granth Sahib serves as an important historical archive. Adherents to related spiritual traditions, the Ravidassias, Kabir-Panthis, and Namdev-Panthis, acknowledge Guru Arjan for preserving works of their foundational saints that might otherwise have been lost. In his epilogue Guru Arjan offers an image for his momentous task: the sacred volume is a *thāl* (large metal dish) with the three dishes of truth (*sat*), contentment (*santokh*), and reflection (*vicār*). These cannot be merely eaten (*khāvai*); they have to be savored (*bhuncai*).

GRANTH APPOINTED AS THE GURU

Just before he passed away in 1708, the tenth Guru terminated the line of personal Gurus and transferred the guruship to the *granth* that now included the compositions of his father, Guru Tegh Bahadar. In the context of his own departure and the politically precarious situation of his community, Guru Gobind Singh's appointment of the *granth* as the Guru would have empowered his Sikhs. Their historical and spiritual past was embodied in the *granth*. The guruship of the *granth* would also resolve any problems of succession posed by schismatic groups. In Sikh memory, Guru Gobind Singh followed the precedent of the first Guru. He placed a five paise coin and a coconut before the *granth* in veneration and bade the gathered Sikhs to henceforth acknowledge the *granth* in his place; there would be no other Guru. His widow, Mata Sundari, strongly pronounced the identity of the Guru and the *granth*: "the Guru is lodged in the word – *gurū kā nivās sabad vicu hai*." Ever since, the Guru Granth Sahib has unequivocally been Sikhs' sole sovereign. The currents of the Guru Granth Sahib are also strongly present in Guru Gobind Singh's *amrit* initiation as the *amrit* is prepared to the accompaniment of Guru Nanak's Japji and Guru Amar

Das's Anand, along with Guru Gobind Singh's Jāp (pronounced with a long "a"), Swayyai, and Chaupai compositions.[4]

Moreover, every morning and evening, Sikhs stand to recite the liturgical *ardās* in unison: "Know the revered Guru Granth is the visible body the Gurus; those who want to meet the Divine, they do so in the numinous word."

NOTES

1 See the research paper "Contemporary Sources of Sikh History (1469–1708)," presented by Dr. Ganda Singh at the Indian History Congress, Khalsa College, Amritsar. Available at https://issuu.com/sikhdigitallibrary/docs/contemporary_sources_of_sikh_histor.
2 Ronki Ram, "Ravidass, Dera Sachkhand Ballan and the Question of Dalit Identity in Punjab," *Journal of Punjab Studies* 16, no. 1 (2008): 7.
3 Eleanor Nesbitt, "'Deg tegh fateh!' Metal as Material and Metaphor in Sikh Tradition," in *Soulless Matter, Seats of Energy – Metals, Gems and Minerals in South Asian Traditions*, ed. Fabrizio Ferrari and Thomas Dähnhardt (London: Equinox, 2016), 174–200.
4 For details see Nikky-Guninder Kaur Singh, "Guru Granth: The Quintessential Sikh Metaphor," *Postscripts: The Journal of Sacred Texts & Contemporary Worlds* 4, no. 2 (2008).

REFERENCES AND FURTHER READING

Mann, Gurinder Singh. *The Making of Sikh Scripture*. New York: Oxford University Press, 2001.

McLeod, W.H. *Guru Nanak and the Sikh Religion*. Oxford: Clarendon, 1968.

Rinehart, Robin. *Debating the Dasam Granth*. New York: Oxford University Press, 2011.

Singh, Harbans. *Guru Nanak and Origins of the Sikh Faith*. Bombay: Asia Publishing House, 1969.

Singh, Nikky-Guninder Kaur. *The First Sikh: Life and Legacy of Guru Nanak*. New Delhi: Penguin Viking, 2019.

Singh, Pashaura. *Life and Work of Guru Arjan: History, Memory, and Biography in the Sikh Tradition*. New Delhi: Oxford University Press, 2006.

Singh, Pashaura. *The Guru Granth Sahib: Canon, Meaning and Authority*. New Delhi: Oxford University Press, 2000.

Singh, Pashaura. *The Routledge Companion to the Life and Legacy of Guru Hargobind*. New Delhi: Routledge, 2024.

2

A HISTORICAL OVERVIEW FROM THE POST-GURU PERIOD TO MODERN TIMES

INTRODUCTION

Sikhs' history from 1708 to the present day can be told with particular reference to religion and literature, to politics and warfare, or to economic and social developments. The narrative in this chapter combines all these strands. At the same time, it is the city of Amritsar and, in particular, its spiritual heart, Harmandar Sahib, and the closely associated Akāl Takht, that will provide a recurrent motif in examining Sikhs' experience from the early 18th century until the present day.

As the previous chapter showed, Amritsar was pivotal to how three Gurus, Guru Ram Das, his son Guru Arjan Dev, and grandson Guru Hargobind, shaped the development of the Sikh religious movement in the 16th and early 17th centuries. Subsequently, Amritsar's history was inseparably caught up, first, in the violent turbulence and the persecution of Sikhs in the 18th century, then, in the first half of the 19th century, in the rise of Sikh confidence during the relative stability and prosperity of the Sikh empire of Maharaja Ranjit Singh (whose capital was the nearby city of Lahore), and thereafter in Sikhism's continuing evolution as a distinctive faith during the decades of British rule and of India's subsequent independence. Each phase has shaped today's Sikh community and their understanding of their faith and their identity.

DOI: 10.4324/9781003359210-2

In what follows, you may well wonder whether you are reading the history of a world religion or of a regionally based community with a tendency to armed struggle. In fact, however, the experience of being harshly repressed and resiliently combative, not least in the 18th century, is intrinsic to 21st-century Sikhs' sense of themselves as a minority that has been cruelly persecuted and that honors its valiant heroes as *shahīds* (martyrs), and this is a key element in Sikh literature and in artists' religious paintings.[1]

To give some examples of Amritsar's centrality to Sikh affairs, since early in the 18th century, the history of the *panth* (the Sikh community) has been punctuated by ***gurmatā*s** (religious resolutions) announced at Harmandar Sahib by successive gatherings of Khalsa Sikhs, collectively known as **Sarbat Khalsa** – that is, "the whole Khalsa." Amritsar was prominent, too, in the impetus (in the early 20th century) to reform the way that the gurdwaras with a historical connection to the Gurus' lives were being managed. Moreover, it was here in Amritsar that Sikhs' most widely recognized code of discipline, *Sikh Rahit Maryādā*, was published in the mid-20th century and it is here, in Gurdwara Ramsar, that the Guru Granth Sahib continues to be printed, on the site where, tradition tells us, Guru Arjan Dev compiled the Guru Granth Sahib and composed his "hymn of peace," the Sukhmani Sahib.

As we shall see too in chapter 5, nowadays developments in the worldwide Sikh community precipitate rulings from Amritsar on permissible conduct (often regarding respect for the Guru Granth Sahib and behavior in gurdwaras). Moreover, as we will see in chapter 4, every day, Sikhs globally are united by social media in pondering the daily guidance from Harmandar Sahib expressed in the early morning ***hukamnāmā*** (the words of the Guru Granth Sahib that appear at the top of the left-hand page when it has been reverently opened at random).

We will be seeing how Sikhs' religious history has involved continual self-definition in relation to the Hindu and Islamic traditions and to other Sikhs whose understanding and emphases differ from their own. Contributing to this ongoing process has been the tension between the Khalsa, comprised of initiated Sikhs bearing the outward signifiers of their allegiance, the Five

Ks, and, on the other hand, self-defined Sikhs bearing few, if any, of the external signs and often combining aspects of an older, broader Indic religiosity with more specifically Sikh observance. At the same time, self-definition as Sikh involves divergent viewpoints among Khalsa Sikhs too, as well as the emergence of significant individuals and their followings and the resultant controversies (see chapters 5 and 7).

An account of Sikh literature from the early 18th century to the present would need to include the successive ***rahitnāmā***s (codes of discipline), including, for example, the probably mid-18th-century Chaupa Singh *rahitnāmā* and the mid-19th-century Prem Sumarag. Over the years, in a number of languages, Sikhs have produced a range of more secular literature too – drama, novels, poetry, autobiography – and chapter 6 will consider this ever-growing body of creative writing.

Politically, Sikhs' history has surged forward from 18th-century friction with invading Islamic overlords, through a period of unification and consolidation during the ascendancy of Maharaja Ranjit Singh and then accommodation to rule by the British and, finally, mounting resistance to it. Since 1947, Sikh history has been intrinsic to the story of independent India. It has included the ambitions of Sikh political parties and calls for greater autonomy from central government, as Sikhs have self-defined in resistance to a majoritarian state and, increasingly, in reaction to mounting Hindu nationalism. At the same time, Sikhs' presence outside India has strengthened numerically (as outlined in chapter 5) as well as being increasingly recognized both locally and nationally. In the 2020s, probably over 3 million Sikhs live outside India and over 23 million in India, of whom around 75 percent live in Punjab. Unfortunately, there are no firm figures as, at the time of writing, there has been no Indian census data since 2011. What is clear is that for a number of reasons, the percentage of Sikhs in Punjab is decreasing.

After reading this chapter and in view of the emphasis on gender equality that Sikhs proclaim, you may well ask, "Where were the women?" Even after some decades of effort in uncovering women's contribution to Sikh history and despite the outstanding bravery of Guru Gobind Singh's supporter, Mai Bhago (Mai means "mother"), during these centuries far fewer women than men have been honored in their lifetime or escaped subsequent anonymity. Even so, as we will see, early in the 18th century, the decisive leadership of Guru Gobind Singh's widow, Mata Sundari (d. 1747), is still remembered.

CONFLICT AND CONFLICT RESOLUTION

To go back to Mata Sundari's period and, more specifically, to the years following the death of Guru Gobind Singh: by 1721 the ***granthī*** (custodian) of Harmandar Sahib was Bhai Mani Singh (1644–1738), who had been a distinguished associate of both Guru Gobind Singh and of his three predecessors. According to Sikh tradition it was here at Harmandar Sahib, at the time of the Baisakhi festival in 1721, that Mani Singh settled a conflict between what had emerged as the two rival factions of the Khalsa – the Tat Khalsa and the Bandai Khalsa. The Tat Khalsa comprised Sikhs who were unswervingly loyal to Guru Gobind Singh whereas the Bandai Khalsa's Sikhs championed Gobind Singh's military successor, Banda Singh Bahadar (1670–1716) and endorsed a rule of conduct that included strict vegetarianism, wearing red clothes – rather than the usual Khalsa color of blue – plus greeting each other with the words "Fateh Darshan, Fateh Dharam" (literally, victory to glimpsing the divine and victory to right conduct) instead of the traditional Khalsa salutation of "Waheguru Ji ka Khalsa, Waheguru Ji ki Fateh" (the Khalsa belongs to God, victory too is God's). Most unacceptably of all to Tat Khalsa Sikhs, Banda Singh had let his followers treat him as a Guru, even though, as we have seen, in 1708 it was the sacred volume of scripture, Guru Granth Sahib, that received in perpetuity the title and role of Guru. So who was Banda Singh and what was the basis of his authority over so many Sikhs?

Banda Singh's title "Bahadar" expressed his reputation for courage in battle. Born into a Hindu family, as a young man he joined an ascetic religious order. Guru Gobind's first encounter with him may well have been in Nanded, in Maharashtra. Certainly, at some point, the Hindu ascetic, previously known as Madho Das, had become Banda Singh, a warrior devoted to Guru Gobind Singh. After his Guru's death, it was Banda

Singh's army that established Khalsa rule in Punjab and he had coins minted in the name of Guru Nanak and Guru Gobind Singh. Banda's soldiers captured Samana, the home of the men responsible for executing Guru Tegh Bahadar and also Guru Gobind Singh's two younger sons, and they then seized Sirhind where the sons' brutal deaths had actually taken place. Moreover, in defiance of the manifestly unjust *zamīndāri* system, whereby feudal landlords oppressed the struggling peasant farmers, Banda Singh restored the land to the agriculturalists themselves. Ultimately, however, his resistance to the Mughals ended humiliatingly in the village of Gurdaspur Nangal: the canal that his men had dug to stop the advance of the imperial forces effectively enabled those forces to besiege Banda Singh's men and starve them into agreeing to their commander's treacherous offer of interceding for them with the emperor. In 1715 Banda Singh was captured and gruesomely tortured to death, but the passionate loyalty of his followers, the Bandai Khalsa, was undiminished and the folk memory of his liberating rebellion has lived on. So too have pressures for agrarian reform and tendencies to factionalism and to both idealizing and idolizing charismatic leaders.

Predictably, Banda Singh's followers' departures from Khalsa protocol were completely unacceptable to many stalwart Sikhs. Led by Guru Gobind Singh's widow, Mata Sundari, these opponents of the Bandai Khalsa assumed for themselves the title of Tat (i.e., pure or true) Khalsa. The conflict that Bhai Mani Singh was to resolve at Harmandar Sahib came to a head after the assassination of the Mughal emperor Farrukh Siyar in 1719. Mughal persecution of the Sikhs then reduced sufficiently for Sikhs to be able to meet from time to time in Amritsar, just as they had done in the years before the persecution. The Tat Khalsa, however, refused the Bandai Khalsa's demand for half the income from the donations that were made at Harmandar Sahib. Indeed, this was what had initially stirred Mata Sundari to dispatch Bhai Mani Singh, together with six other Sikhs, to manage Harmandar Sahib. She ruled that the gurdwara's entire income should be given neither to the Bandai Khalsa nor to the Tat Khalsa but for the provision of food, the *langar*. In April 1721 the Bandai Khalsa was preparing for a fight, but both factions agreed to accept mediation by such a respected personage as Bhai Mani Singh. Mata Sundari's role at this critical time must not be underestimated.

According to Sikh tradition, Bhai Mani Singh's method was to take two pieces of paper, one inscribed with the Bandai Khalsa salutation and the other with the Tat Khalsa salutation. Both slips were then dropped into the *sarovar* (the pool surrounding the gurdwara), and as the first to surface was the Tat Khalsa's "Waheguruji ka Khalsa Waheguruji ki fateh," many Bandai Khalsa supporters switched sides. The schism finally ended when, in front of the Akāl Takht, a wrestler representing the Tat Khalsa defeated his opponent who represented the Bandai Khalsa. Then, coinciding with Divālī in 1723 and in the absence of a leader, the Sarbat Khalsa met in acknowledgment that Mani Singh's intervention and guidance had averted a clash between the Tat Khalsa and the Bandais – although it did not prevent the recurrent fission thereafter into rival religious, military, and political groupings.

In 1726 Amritsar hosted another historic meeting of the Sarbat Khalsa, and in 1733, at yet another gathering, the Sarbat Khalsa accepted two honors from Zakaria Khan, the Mughal governor of Lahore. He had by now realized that the Sikhs were a force to be taken seriously and so had decided to make conciliatory moves – the offer of a nawabship (nawab was a distinguished title) plus a *jagīr* (estate), which would yield revenue, and also permission for Sikhs to have unlimited access to Harmandar Sahib. A highly respected Sikh, Kapur Singh, accordingly accepted the proffered title of Nawab, and from now on, he and, increasingly, another prominent Sikh, Jassa Singh Ahluwalia, were the Sikhs' leaders.

Only a few years later, however, Mani Singh's ongoing role at Harmandar Sahib played a part in his brutal death in 1738, a death that illustrates the continuing repression and persecution of Sikhs at the hands of Zakaria Khan. Mani Singh had sought his permission for Sikhs to celebrate Divālī at Harmandar Sahib and he had agreed to pay Zakaria Khan the tribute of 5,000 rupees that he demanded. (Mani Singh was sure that he could collect the money from the Sikhs who would be coming to celebrate.) Sadly, in the event, he was unable to pay the 5,000 rupees because an imminent military threat from Zakaria Khan's men had deterred Sikhs from actually assembling and, according to Sikh tradition, Zakaria Khan then had Bhai Mani Singh butchered to death by being dismembered, starting with the severing of his wrists. Nonetheless, undeterred by the savage reprisals (capture and death), Sikhs continued undaunted to make pilgrimages to Amritsar, their preeminent shrine.

Harmandar Sahib itself has continued to be central to Sikhs' political and military history. At momentous junctures, throughout the 18th century and indeed up to the present day, it has provided the venue for Sarbat Khalsa assemblies. For instance, after Zakaria Khan's death in 1745, the Sarbat Khalsa assembled at Divālī and resolved to restructure the Sikhs' active fighting force into 25 *jatha*s (bands), each consisting of about 100 men and all under the command of Nawab Kapur Singh. During that same year, not only were some Sikhs in Lahore beheaded, but the *sarovar* of Harmandar Sahib was filled with rubbish to desecrate the holy site. In 1746 in an escalation of violent oppression, Sikhs died in what is known as the ***chota-ghallūghārā*** (smaller massacre). *Ghallūghārā* is often translated by Sikhs as "holocaust" to convey the enormity of the suffering.

Then in accordance with the subsequent *gurmatā* that was pronounced on Baisakhi 1748, the 65 *jathā*s were organized into the Dal Khalsa (Sikh army), in practice a loose confederacy made up of 12 divisions. The name for these divisions was ***misl*** (literally "file"). Although they held sway over different geographic areas and were in competition with each other, the *misl*s would also combine forces in defense of the Khalsa when it was threatened.

And threatened it repeatedly was – by a total of nine Afghan invasions between 1747 and 1769. In Amritsar's history of atrocities and heroism, the name of Baba Dīp Singh, a *misl* leader, stands out. In 1757 the Afghan invader Ahmad Shah Durrani destroyed Harmandar Sahib and desecrated the *sarovar*. Baba Dīp Singh died in the Battle of Amritsar that ensued. He lives on in Sikh hearts and hagiography and, memorably, in iconography, as he is usually depicted bearing his severed head in his hand in his attempt to reach the sacred precincts. Yet again, in 1762 and in 1766–1767, Ahmad Shah invaded the Sikh confederacy, besieged Amritsar, massacred the populace, and destroyed the city. The horrific assault on Sikhs and their holiest shrine in 1762 is remembered as the *vaḍḍā* (big) *ghallūghārā*.

Despite the recurrent destruction, the Sikhs always set to work on reconstruction, and by 1776 Harmandar Sahib's present structure, a harmonious blend of Islamic and Hindu architecture, together with its entrance causeway and connecting bridge, was complete, though without any marble or gilding.

MAHARAJA RANJIT SINGH

The confederacy consisted of *misl*s and Amritsar was the headquarters for the Bhangi *misl*, the largest, most extensive, and most powerful of the *misl*s. However, it was Ranjit Singh (1780–1839), the chief of another *misl*, the Sukarchakia *misl*, who, by the age of 21, was maharaja of Punjab. He had not only defeated the Bhangi *misl* but, through his military leadership, and also by means of his strategic marriages, he had also succeeded in uniting other *misl*s under his authority, although six *misl*s to the south of the Satluj River became British protectorates.[2] For example, Sada Kaur, the mother of his first wife, Mehtab Kaur, succeeded her own father-in-law as leader of the Kanhaiya *misl* and played a key role in consolidating Sikh power in Punjab. Ranjit Singh became ruler of the whole of Punjab to the west of the Satluj River. The "Sikh Empire" of about 12 million people was his creation and it was to survive only ten years after his death.

In the first decades of the 19th century, the increasingly powerful British East India Company, a joint-stock company founded in London in 1600, was the major force to be reckoned with in the subcontinent. As early as 1809 the Treaty of Amritsar formalized an agreement between the maharaja and Charles Metcalfe, representing the company, whereby Ranjit Singh agreed not to expand his realm to the south of the Satluj River. Instead, he consolidated his power farther west.

On gaining control of Amritsar in 1801, Ranjit Singh had announced his intention of renovating Harmandar Sahab. The actual work of reconstruction in marble and copper took place in 1809. So the reason that Harmandar Sahib has been best known, to non-Sikhs at least, for nearly 200 years as the Golden

Temple is that in 1830, to complete his refurbishment of the building, Maharaja Ranjit Singh provided about 162 kilograms of gold to overlay the upper part of the structure with 24-carat gold leaf. Embossed on the gilded copper panel above the shrine's main entrance is an inscription (in Gurmukhi script) recording Ranjit Singh's benefaction in 1830. It reads, "The Great Guru in his wisdom looked upon Maharaja Ranjit Singh as his chief servitor and Sikh, and in his benevolence bestowed on him the privilege of serving the temple." Above these words is the ***mūl mantar***, Guru Nanak's germinal opening words in the Guru Granth Sahib (to be explored in chapter 3).

Just eight years later, in the winter of 1838, the by now ailing Ranjit Singh took his guests Lord Auckland (the British governor general of India) and his sisters, Emily and Fanny Eden, to "the famous Sikh temple, where he had consulted the oracle about his present alliance with us."[3] Emily Eden recorded enthusiastically, and with an oblique reference to the reputed splendor of the Jewish King Solomon's temple 28 centuries earlier in Jerusalem: "The temple is of pure gold, really and truly covered completely with gold, most beautifully carved, till within eight feet from the ground, and then there are panels of marble inlaid with flowers and birds – very Solomonish altogether."[4]

Eden vividly captures Ranjit Singh's enthusiasm and curiosity – whether for the horses he was gifted by King William IV or for the young Queen Victoria's painting that Eden had done as a gift for him. As the painting was being carried, "all the English stood up, and a salute of twenty-one guns was fired. Runjeet took it up in his hands, though it was a great weight, and examined it for at least five minutes with his one piercing eye, and asked for an explanation of the orb and sceptre, and whether the dress were correct, and if it were really like."[5] Eden is also taken by the Sikh maharaja's interest in Christianity: "Runjeet has got a fit of curiosity about our religion. . . . he wants to have translations . . . asked a great many questions about our prayers etc."[6] Again, "Runjeet has been extremely curious about our Sundays and Christmas-days."[7]

When he transgressed in his personal life by marrying Moran, a Muslim dancer, or (according to another narrative) by visiting her before paying his respects in Harmandar Sahib, Ranjit Singh humbly accepted the rebuke from the Akāl Takht. Moreover, it was the Guru Granth Sahib enthroned in Harmandar Sahib that he consulted as an "oracle" before undertaking any military venture. Emily Eden's nephew, William Osborne, described Ranjit Singh's "very simple method of solving his doubts, by placing between the leaves of the Grunth [*sic*] two slips of paper, on one of which is written the object of his wishes, and on the other the reverse."[8] Osborne explained that one of Ranjit's "Gooroos or priests" would then pick one, without looking at it, and on this basis he would either undertake an expedition very confidently or would abandon it forthwith.

The maharaja's generous endowment encouraged many other patrons to make donations, among them the (Muslim) nizam of Hyderabad who began making yearly grants to the Golden Temple. Ranjit Singh was responsible not only for the rebuilding and enhancement of Harmandar Sahib in Amritsar but also for reconstructing other historic gurdwaras and, indeed, the construction of Hindu temples and Muslim mosques. Among the historic gurdwaras is Takht Sri Patna Sahib, marking Guru Gobind Singh's birthplace in Patna in the Indian state of Bihar; Takht Hazur Sahib, marking the place where he died in Nanded in the state of Maharashtra; and the gurdwara in Nankana Sahib, near Lahore in Pakistan, commemorating Guru Nanak's birth there in 1469.

In the religious demography of his empire, Sikhs were a minority (only 10 percent) and Muslims and Hindus constituted the bulk of the population. Ranjit Singh was respectful of all religious communities and extended his patronage equally to his Muslim, Hindu, and Sikh subjects, and they all held important positions in diverse areas of his kingdom. The language of his court was Persian, which had been the official language of the Mughal emperors since the time of Akbar. Even the first coins struck by the Sikh king were in the Persian script. He fostered the celebration of Hindu and Muslim festivals, and respectful of Hindu sentiments, he prohibited the slaughter of cows.

It has to be recognized too that while Ranjit Singh is sometimes idealized as a Sikh hero, Muslim historians' accounts are less fulsome. He is also criticized by those Sikhs who regard monarchy as a departure from the Khalsa principles of a Sikh republic. What is not in question is his military success and diplomacy. From the age of ten, Ranjit Singh had fought in battle and it was his part in defeating Afghan invaders that had propelled him to prominence. Later on, as supreme ruler of the Sikh empire, he led Sikh, Hindu, Muslim, and European soldiers and, indeed, it was his French and Italian advisers who enabled him to modernize the army. He won their respect and that of the British. Scottish colonial explorer Alexander Burnes (a great-nephew of the poet Robert Burns) who spent two months in Lahore (1831) praises the maharaja for his penetrating intelligence and exemplary humanity (as did Emily Eden and other European visitors). "Ranjeet Sing is, in every respect, an extraordinary character. I have heard his French officers observe that he has no equal from Constantinople to India; and all of them have seen the intermediate powers," records Burnes.[9]

The nearly four decades of Maharaja Ranjit Singh's rule are acclaimed for his pluralistic rule and for modernization and prosperity. The arts and crafts flourished, not least due to his patronage of exquisite embellishment of Harmandar Sahib. Notably – and unusually at that time in Europe as well as Asia – there was no death penalty under Maharaja Ranjit Singh.

SIKH-BRITISH INTERACTION

Increasingly, it was Sikh relations with the British, rather than with the Mughals and other Muslim invaders and oppressors, that shaped Sikh history. Following Ranjit Singh's death in 1839, the British were quick to see the vulnerability of the Sikh kingdom as one of his successors after another was murdered. In the two Anglo-Sikh Wars (1845–1846 and 1848–1849) Sikh soldiers impressed the British with their courage and tenacity, but the treachery of their leaders in the first war prevented a Sikh victory, which might well have changed the course of not only Sikh history, and indeed of Indian history, but also of British imperial history.

Just one of Ranjit Singh's acknowledged heirs, Duleep Singh, who was the youngest, survived, and as a boy of ten, in 1849 he signed the Last Treaty of Lahore whereby the British East India Company annexed Punjab. The Lahore court's most celebrated treasure, the Koh-i-Noor diamond, was gifted to Queen Victoria. Maharaja Duleep Singh's mother, Maharani Jind Kaur, who was vilified by her British detractors, is one of Sikh history's most spirited and high-profile personalities.

After annexing Punjab, the British had an impact on Sikh life in a number of ways. Their preferred recruits for the British Indian Army were men from what the British defined as "martial races." Sikhs, like the Gurkhas from Nepal, were a prime example of these. Serving as a soldier provided a salary and also opened up the possibility of overseas travel, initially to East Asia but, in the First World War, to Western Europe and other theaters of war. As Sikh recruits were expected by their British masters to be initiated into the Khalsa and to maintain the Five Ks, and as *granthīs* were employed to accompany Sikh regiments, the Sikh soldiers' army life and religious adherence were integrated.

Christian missionaries too influenced the Sikhs' religious history. As early as 1813 the Charter Act had contained a clause permitting missionaries to operate in India. The effort to convert Indians to Christianity gained in momentum throughout the 19th century. The first Presbyterian missionaries, John Cameron Lowrie and William Reed, reached Punjab in 1834, and the American Presbyterian Mission's first station was established in Ludhiana. Following Punjab's annexation in 1849, Church Missionary Society missions were established in the 1850s in Amritsar and Lahore.[10] Amritsar, rather than Lahore, was chosen as the site of the first mission in Punjab because it was "the native centre of the Sikh race."[11] Moreover, the missionaries regarded Sikhs as especially ripe for conversion and sometimes even ventured into gurdwaras to preach. Although the appeal of Christianity was strongest for Sikhs from the most disadvantaged communities, the missionaries also won a few royal converts. Not only was Maharaja Ranjit's son Duleep Singh baptized as a Christian, but in 1853 several members of Kapurthala's princely family also became Christian.

Christians provided medical care and established schools, and this, together with their evangelizing, was a spur to concerned Sikhs, Muslims, and Hindus to reform and energize their own faith communities. To accompany their hymn singing, the missionaries also introduced the harmonium, which Sikhs and

Hindus proceeded to adopt for their own devotional purposes, and the missionaries brought the latest communications technology, the printing press. The Christians' Ludhiana Mission Press employed a Gurmukhi typeface which would in time greatly increase the circulation of materials published by Sikhs as well as enabling the Guru Granth Sahib to be printed in 1864. At the same time, the print matter that now became available in Punjab in the Devanagari script and the Arabic script, as well as in Gurmukhi, accentuated the difference between Hindus, Muslims, and Sikhs.

Both British legislation and the implementation of the decennial census also impacted Sikh society. One law enforced a social division between Sikhs of different castes and another hardened the distinction between Hindus and Sikhs. The census required everyone to enter their caste and their religious allegiance, so making Sikhs more aware than ever of their minority status.

In 1862, a century after the *vaḍḍā ghallūghārā*, construction began of an architecturally totally inappropriate Gothic clock tower which would dominate Harmandar Sahib until the tower was demolished in 1945. It stood as an unwelcome reminder of the insensitivity of British rule. However, moves were soon afoot for Sikhs to regain control over their historical gurdwaras from their government-supported custodians, the *mahant*s, as well as for Indians more generally to achieve home rule.

SIKH REFORM MOVEMENTS

Three movements of Sikh renewal had emerged in the late 19th century some decades before the early 20th-century campaign to put management of gurdwaras firmly in Sikh hands. These were the **Nirankaris**, the **Namdharis** (also known as Kukas), and the **Singh Sabha** movement. Although the Nirankaris and Namdharis faced criticism from other Sikhs for believing in the necessity of having a living human Guru, their contribution to the mainstream was significant. Using the name "Nirankar" (formless), one of Guru Nanak's words for the universal Divine, the Nirankaris' founder, Dayal Das (1783–1855), exhorted Sikhs to worship the formless God and so to desist from worshipping images of deities, from going on pilgrimages and from patronizing rites that were conducted by Brahmins. According to Nirankari tradition at least, today's Sikh marriage ceremony, ***anand kāraj***, which is centered on the enthroned Guru Granth Sahib (rather than on a sacred fire), owes its origins to their movement.

The Namdharis' founding figures were Balak Singh (1799–1862) and his successor Ram Singh (b. 1816). (According to Namdhari tradition, he did not die, although British sources record his death in exile in Myanmar in 1885.) Namdhari discipline entailed strict vegetarianism, simple clothing, and inexpensive marriages, and Namdharis took other steps too to improve women's education and standing. Decades before Gandhi's campaign for self-rule, Namdharis were boycotting British institutions such as the postal service. Important though the Namdhari and Nirankari initiatives were, modern Sikhism owes more to the Singh Sabha movement which combined resistance to British rule with zeal to cleanse Sikhism of Hindu elements and to put an end to corrupt practices. Among other things, this meant the recasting of life cycle rites, and in 1909 the Anand Marriage Act duly recognized Sikhs' distinctive ceremony. Also thanks to the Singh Sabha, new emphasis was placed on Punjabi language and culture.

The historical designation of "Tat Khalsa" resurfaced, certainly from about 1911, this time being applied by others to the dominant Singh Sabha faction in Lahore. The Lahore Singh Sabha had been founded in 1879 to rival the Amritsar Singh Sabha which continued to be comfortable with a style of Sikhism that honored – to the extent of worshipping – Guru Nanak's descendants, members of the Bedi family, and was unconcerned about the Hindu practices of many Sikhs. The name Tat Khalsa denoted Sikhs with a full commitment to action on behalf of the Sikh community, in contrast to *ḍhillaṛ*, or "indolent, passive, ineffectual" Sikhs.

The leader of the Lahore Singh Sabha was Gurmukh Singh, a professor. He established contact with Kahn Singh Nabha, a notable scholar, who produced, first, *Mahan Kosh* (an encyclopedia of Sikhism that is still in use and highly regarded) and then *Ham Hindu Nahin* (We are not Hindus). What instigated this public assertion was the pressure of a Hindu reformist organization, the Arya Samaj, which was actively recruiting in

Punjab. Kahn Singh Nabha's pamphlet was published in Amritsar by the Wazir Hind Press. Subsequently he and Gurmukh Singh offered guidance to an Irish divisional judge, Max Arthur Macauliffe, as he worked on the first English rendering of the Guru Granth Sahib to win acceptance by Sikhs, a task that he completed in 1909. (An earlier partial translation that had been commissioned by the British government was rejected by Sikhs as disrespectful.)

JALLIANWALA BAGH

In December 1919, a year after the end of the First World War in which thousands of Sikh soldiers had served and lost their lives, Amritsar was mentioned in a British newspaper. The *Manchester Guardian*'s headline read, "An astonishing story from India: Punjab meeting dispersed by fire in April troubles. Over 400 natives killed: Three times as many wounded."[12] It had in fact been eight months earlier, on the day of the Baisakhi festival, that the then–brigadier general Reginald Dyer had ordered his men to open fire on the crowd, including many Sikhs, who had gathered in Jallianwala Bagh, an enclosed public space. The massacre was the lowest point in Britain's century of colonial rule. It is noteworthy that it was only brought to the British public's attention at all after an inquiry had been held. Downplayed though it was in the British media, the Amritsar massacre marked a turning point in Indians' mounting campaign for independence.

What few people realized either at the time or subsequently was how narrowly Harmandar Sahib itself escaped being damaged or even destroyed in the unrest. In April 1919 Melicent Wathen, an English botanical artist, the wife of Gerard Wathen, the principal of Khalsa College in Amritsar, recorded in her journal the role her husband had played: "Martial law proclaimed at Amritsar and Lahore. Gerard was at least able to dissuade Dyer from authorizing a bombardment from the air the next day. If anything happened to the Golden Temple, he said, it would permanently alienate the Sikhs and therefore a large proportion of the Indian Army."[13] Nonetheless, on 14th April an aerial attack was ordered on the neighboring district of Gujranwala.

REGAINING CONTROL OF HISTORICAL SACRED SITES

In Amritsar the next year, a meeting took place near Akāl Takht with the purpose of electing a representative committee to administer Harmandar Sahib and other gurdwaras of historical importance. This committee was named the **Shiromani Gurdwara Parbandhak Committee** (Chief Gurdwara Management Committee), though it is more often referred to by its acronym, **SGPC**, and its aim was to replace the gurdwaras' current (in some cases corrupt) custodians, the *mahant*s. Reformist Sikhs formed *jathā*s (bands of men) who occupied each historical gurdwara in turn. Collectively, the concerted action to restore gurdwaras to Sikh management is known both as the gurdwara reform movement and the Akālī movement. Like "Tat Khalsa," the name "**Akālī**" was already resonant with history – *akālī* was the name of Guru Gobind Singh's fearless fighters and it was a reminder too of Akāl Purakh, the Timeless One.

Some *mahant*s ceded control peacefully, but in some major gurdwaras, such as Tarn Taran near Amritsar and at Guru Nanak's birthplace, Nankana Sahib, the struggle became violent. Eventually, the legislation that was passed in 1925 meant that by the terms of the Sikh Gurdwaras Act, control of Punjab's historical gurdwaras was finally handed over to the SGPC.

Sikh discipline more generally also called for an overhaul. Many *rahitnāmā*s (codes of conduct) had been produced in the 18th and 19th centuries, each listing requirements and prohibitions, whether regarding permitted foods, clothing, necessary haircare or procedures for initiation, marriage, birth or funerals. In 1927 the SGPC appointed a subcommittee tasked with drawing up a new code of conduct for Sikhs. The subcommittee's 29 members included distinguished Sikh scholars (among them Bhai Kahan Singh Nabha and the literary pioneer Bhai Vir Singh) who had been influenced by the Singh Sabha and Akāli movements. Moreover, the Shiromani Akāli Dal and over 20 other Sikh organizations commented on drafts before the *Sikh Rahit Maryādā* was published in 1950 under the auspices of the Akāl Takht, the supreme corporate Sikh authority.

GROUPINGS WITHIN THE PANTH

Some groups, however, such as the Namdharis, follow rules that are specific to them rather than adhering to the *Sikh Rahit Maryādā*. The 20th century saw the emergence of a new group too, the Akhand Kirtani Jatha (AKJ), associated with the freedom fighter Bhai Randhir Singh (1878–1961). In accordance with his principles, AKJ members are strictly vegetarian, eating food that has been prepared and served in iron utensils, and women wear a small turban under their scarf. The name Akhand Kirtani Jatha literally means a "continuous singing squad," as one of their distinctive practices is *rain sabāī kīrtan* (all-night singing of the Gurus' hymns). The AKJ's *nām simaran* (spiritual discipline, literally "remembrance of the divine name") consists of nonstop recitation of the divine name Waheguru for an hour each day.

Among other groupings to emerge in the Panth (Sikh community) in the 20th century are the followers of Baba Nand Singh (c. 1870–1943), an ascetic who would, in his humility, meditate below ground level at Nanaksar in Punjab. Followers gather in large numbers for particularly impressive *kīrtan* on each month's full moon night and their veneration of the Guru Granth Sahib is on a much larger scale than in other gurdwaras. Both the AKJ and the Nanaksar tradition continue to flourish as religiously committed, minority strands within the Panth.

SIKHS IN INDEPENDENT INDIA

Before the *Sikh Rahit Maryādā* could be published, Sikhs were profoundly affected by three momentous events: first, the Second World War (1939–1945), then India's attainment of independence from British rule (August 1947), and a few days later, the partition of Punjab between the newly created nation-states of Pakistan and India.

During the Second World War many Sikhs enlisted in the British Indian Army and thousands were killed or injured in battle, many of them in France. Meanwhile hope for home rule intensified. In August 1947, British rule over India came to an end, but the celebrations were short-lived as several million people, including hundreds of thousands of Sikhs, lost their homes, were injured or killed, or in the case of women, suffered sexual violence during the horrors triggered by the announcement of where exactly the line would be drawn between India and the new state of Pakistan. At great risk to their lives, many thousand Sikhs fled as refugees from west of the new border into the now-partitioned India.

CODE OF DISCIPLINE

In 1950 the *Sikh Rahit Maryādā* (Sikh code of conduct) was at last published. The section on individual conduct starts by defining a Sikh as any woman or man believing in (or one could equally well translate the verb used here as "accepting" rather than "believing in") one God, the ten Gurus and their teaching, and the Guru Granth Sahib. A Sikh must also believe in/ accept the importance of *amrit* (initiation) and must not adhere to any other religion. Echoing the words of Guru Ram Das, the *Sikh Rahit Maryādā* states, "A Sikh should rise early, take a bath, and then meditate on the one true God." It lists the scriptural passages for daily reading or recitation (see more about this in chapter 4), and it details the behavior that is appropriate in the gurdwara. This includes the procedure for taking advice from the Guru Granth Sahib and the recipe for the sweet wheat-flour pudding (***kaṛāh prashād***) that worshippers receive. It also prohibits Hindu-style practices, such as ceremonial bell ringing and worship of religious images, as well as any involvement in caste, astrology, and ideas of pollution. Other forbidden practices include cutting children's hair and the use of intoxicants or tobacco, plus infanticide (especially of girls – presumably because male infants weren't subject to infanticide), as well as gambling, stealing, adultery, and child marriage. Life cycle rites are outlined, and Sikhs are exhorted to offer *sevā* (voluntary service). *Langar* (its preparation, service, and consumption) is described both as training people in *sevā* and as overcoming caste distinction.

Matters of community discipline, such as the procedure for initiation (*amrit samchār), tanakhāh* (penance for a disciplinary breach), and *gurmatā* (decision on a religious question) are defined in the much shorter second part of the *Sikh Rahit Maryādā*.

Meanwhile, moves were also afoot to redraw the physical boundaries of Punjab itself. Sikhs' political party, the Shiromani Akāli Dal (which had been founded in 1920 to implement the SGPC's gurdwara reform campaign), now led the Punjabi Suba movement. In a sustained hunger strike Sikhs' leader Master Tara Singh nearly gave his life to the cause. Its aim was to create a Punjab state (*sūbā*) that would correspond more closely to the area in which the mother tongue was Punjabi. In practice this meant creating a Sikh-majority state, given that Hindus whose mother tongue was Punjabi recorded themselves officially as having Hindi as their mother tongue.

A SIKH-MAJORITY STATE

This was achieved in 1966, a year that started auspiciously with the return to the Sikhs of Guru Gobind Singh's weapons by the great-granddaughter of Lord Dalhousie who had acquired them from the Lahore state treasury in 1849 after the Anglo-Sikh Wars.

By the Punjab Reorganisation Act of 1966, a decade after India's other states had been delineated, the modern state of Punjab was formed, the first and only state to have a Sikh majority. At the same time the new state of Haryana was born, while some territory was transferred to the hilly area, Himachal Pradesh. The city of Chandigarh (the capital of both Punjab and Haryana) became a Union Territory. However, this outcome, a truncated Punjab, was a disappointment to the campaigners in several respects.

Consequently, the Akāli Dal continued to agitate for Chandigarh and Punjabi-speaking parts of Haryana to be included in Punjab and their other demands included giving Punjab control of its vital river water, the majority of which was being diverted to supply two other states with water. These were among the demands contained in the Anandpur Sahib Resolution, drafted in 1973 and reformulated in 1978. In 1982 the Akāli Dal launched a Dharam Yudh Morcha (righteous campaign) intended to ensure the implementation of the resolution's demands and aiming at greater devolution for Punjab from the central government as well as claiming Amritsar as Punjab's capital.

1984 AND AFTER

If Baisakhi 1919 in Amritsar had marked the nadir of British rule in India, in 1984, another festival day in Amritsar, this time the *gurpurab* (anniversary of a Guru) in June commemorating Guru Arjan's *shahīdī* (martyrdom) marked the lowest point in Sikhs' relations with the government of independent India. Sixty-five years after the Amritsar massacre, fresh carnage and loss of life – this time perpetrated actually within the sacred precincts and on the orders of India's own government – brought Harmandar Sahib and Akāl Takht to global attention. On 1st June orders were given, on the authority of the prime minister, Indira Gandhi, to remove a charismatic and heavily armed preacher, Jarnail Singh Bhindranwale, and his followers from the precincts. These loyal supporters included four retired army generals and at least 14 retired colonels. The name for this military intervention was Operation Bluestar and it lasted from 1st to 10th June.

During the operation an unknown number of Sikhs were killed. The Akāl Takht was seriously damaged and was rebuilt twice, once under the auspices of the Indian government and then by Sikhs. The whereabouts, and indeed existence, of historical documents and other valued items housed in the original Sikh Reference Library are uncertain as it too was destroyed and the surviving contents were removed by the army.

Jarnail Singh Bhindranwale (1947–1984) was the spiritual leader of Bhindran Taksal, a Sikh religious training center in which he had himself studied. His fiery preaching encouraged his hearers, predominantly rural Sikh men, to turn from drugs and alcohol to their families and Sikh teaching. At the same time, his impassioned rhetoric also called for greater autonomy for Sikhs from central government and for the Anandpur Resolution to be implemented. He had also condemned as heretical the Sant Nirankaris, an offshoot of the older Nirankari movement, who, like them, honored a living Guru. It was following a violent clash between Bhindranwale's followers and Sant Nirankaris on Baisakhi day 1978 that Bhindranwale had taken refuge in Harmandar Sahib and he had subsequently been permitted to live actually inside the Akāl Takht. In an interview in 1984 with a *Sunday Times* journalist, he clarified, "We want nothing less than recognition of the Sikhs as a separate nation."[14]

To Punjab's Hindus and to India's ruling Congress Party, such statements and the Sikh campaign for devolution sounded like a separatist demand for total autonomy, and following the events of 1984, there was indeed mounting Sikh support for **Khalistan**, an independent Sikh state. In November 1984 Indira Gandhi was assassinated by her two Sikh bodyguards. Politically orchestrated violence immediately erupted against Sikhs, principally in Delhi. Thousands of Sikhs disappeared during the months of an Indian army crackdown on suspected "terrorists."

Sikhs internationally were challenged to the core. Their disillusionment with India and their alienation reached an all-time high. The noted Sikh journalist and historian Khushwant Singh urged India's Sikh president, Zail Singh, to resign. Khushwant Singh himself and other distinguished Sikhs returned their prestigious civilian awards. Demands for Khalistan mounted, and violent unrest in Punjab lasted into the 1990s. These demands continue to reverberate in the 2020s, especially in Canada but also in the United Kingdom, Australia, and the United States.

Chapter 7 discusses a number of other 21st-century developments that show the continuing vitality of the Sikh community.

CONCLUDING REFLECTIONS

Reflecting on the life of Jarnail Singh Bhindranwale and on Banda Singh Bahadur and other historical figures in this chapter, it would be all too easy to see Sikhs' history and achievements in terms of violent conflict and of the rise and fall of charismatic militant leaders and to associate Amritsar and its sacred sites primarily with atrocities. This would be to disregard other key aspects of Sikhs' heritage and vocation, as evidenced during the reign of Maharaja Ranjit Singh, and certainly to overlook Sikhs' commitment to compassionate voluntary service (*sevā*), and Sikhs' contribution to agriculture, business, industry, and many other fields.

One notable expression of compassionate *sevā* stands near Amritsar's bus terminus. This is the Pingalwara (home for people with a disability) which was established by one of the 20th century's most inspirational Sikhs, Bhagat Puran Singh

(1904–1992). The All India Pingalwara Charitable Society has grown from Bhagat Puran Singh's decades of tirelessly serving people abandoned by society – many of them mentally challenged or terminally ill.[15] Another compassionate initiative is embodied in Khalsa Aid, founded in the United Kingdom in 1999 by Ravi Singh, which has been followed by a growing number of *sevā* organizations that provide emergency support globally and longer term support locally.

Harmandar Sahib is the most prominent of Sikh pilgrimage sites: it is a magnet for tourists and famed for providing up to 80,000 cooked vegetarian meals a day in its *langar* – increasing to double that amount on festival days. It has also been at the heart of tensions between the impulse to modernize facilities and the need to conserve heritage. These considerations combine too in the creation of Sikh museums, one of the most recent being the Golden Temple Interpretation Centre, a multimedia museum established in 2016 beneath the plaza outside Harmandar Sahib. Rather than conserving and displaying historical artefacts, Sikh museums exhibit modern paintings of key events such as the deaths of "martyrs" with the intention of presenting graphically a contemporary Sikh understanding of history.

The ongoing story of Sikhism is one of utilizing new media while responding to the many pressures and opportunities of modernity, in a spirit of grounded and unflagging optimism, referred to by Sikhs as *chaṛdhī kalā*. It is to the theological and ethical aspects of the Sikh religion that we now turn.

NOTES

1 See chapter 5 and also Louis Fenech, *Martyrdom in the Sikh Tradition: Playing the "Game of Love"* (New York: Oxford University Press, 2005).
2 See Priya Atwal, *Royals and Rebels: The Rise and Fall of the Sikh Empire* (London: Hurst, 2020).
3 Emily Eden, *Up the Country: Letters from India* (London: Virago, [1866] 1997), 215.
4 Eden, *Up the Country*, 215–216.
5 Eden, *Up the Country*, 200.
6 Eden, *Up the Country*, 228.
7 Eden, *Up the Country*, 30.
8 William G. Osborne. *The Court and Camp of Runjeet Sing* [*sic*] (London: Henry Colburn), 122.

9 Alexander Burnes, *Travels into Bokhara: Being the Account of Journey from India to Cabool, Tartary and Persia* (Philadelphia: Carey and Hart, 1835), 116.

10 In 1834 a missionary from the Presbyterian Church in the United States came to Ludhiana. For detail of successive Christian denominations' missionary activity in 19th-century Punjab, see John C. B. Webster, "Punjabi Christians," *Journal of Punjab Studies* 16 (2009): 35–36.

11 *Proceedings of the Church Missionary Society for Africa and the East, One-Hundred-and-Twenty-First Year* (London: Church Missionary Society, 1920), 47.

12 *Manchester Guardian*, December 13, 1919.

13 Melicent Wathen, Diary (Private collection, 1919), cited in Raleigh Trevelyan, *The Golden Oriole* (London: Secker & Warburg, 1987), 483.

14 Mary Anne Weaver, "India's Warring 'Ayatollah' Faces Commando Siege," *Sunday Times*, March 4, 1984, 19.

15 Patwant Singh and Harinder Kaur Sekhon, *Garland around My Neck: The Story of Puran Singh of Pingalwara* (Birmingham, UK: DTF Publishers, 2001).

REFERENCES AND FURTHER READING

Atwal, Priya. *Royals and Rebels: The Rise and Fall of the Sikh Empire.* London: Hurst, 2020.

Mahmood, Cynthia Keppley. *Fighting for Faith and Nation: Dialogues with Sikh Militants.* Philadelphia: University of Pennsylvania Press, 1996.

Rai, Gurmeet S., with Raghu Rai. *Amritsar: A City in Remembrance.* New Delhi: Om Publications, 2021.

Singh, Gurharpal, and Giorgio Shani. *Sikh Nationalism.* Cambridge: Cambridge University Press, 2021.

Wagner, Kim A. *Amritsar 1919: An Empire of Fear and the Making of a Massacre.* New Haven: Yale University Press, 2019.

3

THEOLOGICAL IMAGINARY AND EXISTENTIAL REALITY

Ikkoankār [see figure 3.1] is Guru Nanak's all-inclusive expression for the singular One beyond space, time, cause, or gender. To use the 20th-century French phenomenologist Paul Ricoeur's term, it is the "originary" mode of discourse through which Sikh religion has come to language.[1] This One is named truth (*sat nām*). By naming unicity (oneness), the metaphysical Being is brought into language so that it is actively engaged with; clearly not a doctrinal formulation, truth is to be embodied and lived out in tangible ways. Sikh theology, we claim, is existential, sensuous, world-affirming, all-inclusive, panentheistic – this multiverse is *in* the infinite One, and that One is very much *in* this multiverse. The divine-human intimacy becomes apparent in the following three overlapping segments.

THEOLOGICAL MATRIX: THE *MŪL MANTAR*

Ikkoankār sat nām kartā purakh nirbhao nirvairu akāl mūrat ajūnī saibhan gurprasād is the Sikh theological matrix, popularly called the *mūl mantar*, the quintessential refrain (*mūl* is literally "the root"). This condensed prologue to Guru Nanak's Japji inaugurates the 1,430-page Guru Granth Sahib, prefaces its numerous segments, and is the keynote of daily prayers and ceremonies. Its divine imaginary showcases the integral relationship between theology and its lived dimension. Instead of adopting conventional philosophy of religion categories, we will apply the *mūl mantar*'s own inbuilt framework to introduce Sikh theological perspectives.

DOI: 10.4324/9781003359210-3

ONE BEING (IKKOANKĀR)

The opening configuration, One Being [see figure 3.1], is a visual and verbal invitation to venture out toward the expansive One. The numeral one (1) at the outset is followed by the character in the Gurmukhi script which represents a long "o" sound. As you can see in figure 3.1, it has a geometric arc flying away into space and time.

This combination is recognized as *ikkoankār*. Numerical, alphabetical, and geometrical modes innovatively and rhythmically repeat to unequivocally pronounce the unicity and inclusivity of the One beyond gender demarcations and causal contingencies. While the former two constitute the beginning of the mathematical and verbal languages, the flying arc symbolizes having neither beginning nor end. This is Guru Nanak's expression of the One formless infinite ground of all that exists. By registering the archetypal interior individual journey to ultimate unity, the ubiquitous *oan* at the center highlights the Sikh theological and existential connection. As the Mandukya and Chandogya Upanishads of the earlier Hindu tradition comprehensively explain, Oan/Om/Aum is a fourfold passage from the state of dualistic consciousness to semiconsciousness to unconsciousness to the experience of absolute totality – a unity one is deeply aware of, a unity that one fully enjoys, a unity where the self is totally cognizant of its intrinsic infinite Oneness. The foundational Sikh configuration conjoins an individual's emotional expansion with the infinite singular subject.

Guru Nanak's successors follow his example and the Guru Granth Sahib is replete with the celebration of the one reality. "The One is within the self, the One is without, that One is in every place and interspace" (GGS: 45); "ahead or behind there is only the One" (GGS: 391); "always, always You alone are the One Reality" (GGS: 139). Persian terminology is used to emphasize the unicity of being: "*asti ek digari kuī ek tuī ek tuī* – only the One is, there is none other; only You, You only" (GGS: 143–144). There is

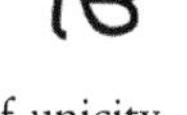

Figure 3.1 Ikkoankār, symbol of unicity

no opposition between the One and the many, nor is there any dualism between unity and plurality: "from the One issue forth the countless and into the One they join" (GGS: 131). Unity becomes plurality and plurality eventually becomes unity.

The utterly formless One is spontaneously embraced by the Guru Granth Sahib authors in a variety of personal relations utilizing a range of terms current in multireligious, multiethnic, multilinguistic Punjab. They depict concrete reciprocal ties in which both sides relate to each other in their immediate presence. Human-divine intimacy is expressed through love between a bride and her groom and through numerous other relationships. The One is imagined as father, mother, brother, friend, and lover. "You are our mother, father, near and far; You permeate each of us" (GGS: 818). Particularly striking is the maternal imaginary. Celebrating the infinite One through the gestation, birthing, and lactation processes the Guru Granth Sahib brings us back to the mother's body and to the bodies in this world we belong to.[2]

The numeral one denotes an inclusive oneness, conjoining the two antithetical categories of medieval Punjab: "Hindus and Muslims have the same One sovereign" (GGS: 1158). Since everything is a manifestation of that One, all the manifestations would be a part of it. Set free from conventional icons and images, the infinite One can be accessed as Allah, Ram, Sita, Nirvana, brother, sister, lover, parent, bee, breeze . . . Sikhism is not a belief system; its leitmotif is intimate love for the One voiced in the "language of infinite love" (*bhākhiā bhāo apāru*) (GGS: 2). The Guru Granth Sahib flows with numerous Arabic-Persian epithets for the divine One. Terms like Khuda, Allah, Rahim, Parvardgar, Meharvan, Haqq, Kabir, Karim, Maula, Rabb, Sahib, and its variation Sahiba familiarize readers with the Islamic characteristics and attributes of the singular One. In the Guru Granth Sahib repertoire, these Arabic and Persian names evoke the infinite one who rejoices within everybody, rather than the customary distant monotheistic godhead of Islam to whom all creatures must submit.

Islamic terms join with Nirvana to express the singular One overflowing everywhere, which is quite different from the

Buddhist "emptiness." Likewise Divine names from the Hindu world which often refer to incarnations are abundantly used in the Guru Granth Sahib to designate the non-incarnate Divine: Hari, Ram, Prabh (also Prabhu and Prabhi), Dharnidhar, Gobind, Murari, Madhoji, Narayana, Paramesaru, Parvadagaru, Pranadhara, Srirang, Vasudeva, and so forth. Understanding these familiar divine names in the Guru Granth Sahib requires a conscious break from our preconceptions and intellectual habits. Its never-ending theological imaginary goes to prove the utter impossibility of imaging the formless One (*nirankār*) in any particular form. No god, no body, and no thing could ever be excluded from the all-pervasive One.

The open-armed arc of *ikkoankār* welcomes men and women, literate or illiterate, to feel the one they are familiar with – to feel that infinite One physically within (*antar*) and all around (*bāhar*), to feel that One spatially and temporally behind (*pichai*) and ahead (*agai*). The Sikh theological One is an inner, subjective experience of infinity here on earth rather than an objective knowledge of or belief in one God beyond.

*TRUTH ITS NAME (*SAT NĀM)

Truth is *the* name of that One, and all other names are Its aspects. Evidently 15th-century North India was abuzz with eloquent terms and philosophically sophisticated concepts from Sanskrit, Arabic, and Persian. Guru Nanak's choice of giving the One the name of truth (*sat*) reiterates the absolute unity and inclusivity of the numeral one. Shared across celestial, terrestrial, and nether worlds, truth has no spatial or temporal limits; it has no demarcations male or female, no designations, no color, no form. The name (*nām) sat* gestures infinite movement, "existing," "occurring," "happening," "being present." The indissoluble relationship between the infinite ontological "one" and its total expression "truth" sustains the Sikh cosmological, philosophical, social, and moral world: "everything is truth – *saco sac*" (GGS: 1289). Truth is not exclusive to any one religion or any one name. Truth does not hold on to any existing form of god or doctrine nor is it bound by any monotheistic, polytheistic, monistic, pantheistic, or heno-theistic category. Besides the Indic term *sat*, the Islamic, Arabic term *haqq* (similarly meaning "truth") also appears in the Guru Granth Sahib.

The first stanza of Guru Nanak's Japji underscores the ever-present reality in the fluctuations of time: "Truth was in the beginning, truth has been through the cycles, truth is, says Nanak, and truth will be ever more" (GGS: 1). Instead of the usual triple tenses of time, there is an additional fourth as truth in the past has two dimensions: primal absolute truth before the beginning of time (*ādi sac*) and truth participating in the alternate cycles of creation and dissolution (yugas/*jugād sac*). These two are balanced with the present "is" (*hai bhī sac*) and the future "will be" (*hosī bhī sac*). Functioning in and through the various tenses of time, timeless truth validates each instant in this fleeting world. The phenomenal world is the fullness and reality of the singular truth.

We do come across a quick shift from the infinite formless One named Truth (*sat*/*sac*) to the temporal, spatial, physical individual living truthfully (*saciārā*). "How to *be* true – *kiv saciārā hoi e?*" (GGS: 1). The metaphysical truth must be lived experientially. The Japji question incites self-critique: what attitudes, actions, proclivities prevent living truthfully? It is followed up by another existential question: "How to break the walls of falsity?" The visual image spells out the urgency of breaking false dualistic constructs inhibiting the feel of unicity. Ultimately, in Sikh theology, "those who reflect on Truth are true themselves." The three dishes on the scriptural platter we may recall (chapter 1) are truth, contentment, and reflection which must be aesthetically relished. The ontological truth is an all-embracing *becoming* that flows in the cosmos and seeps into the human world of motions and emotions. Not an abstract concept, truth is practically lived out in the daily rhythms of this temporal world. The penultimate stanza of the Japji states, "In the realm of truth dwells the formless One," and the Sikh goal is to the enter this realm, a concurrence of the individual and the Divine.

*CREATOR PERSON (*KARTĀ PURAKH)

The lexical juxtaposition of *sat nām* (truth its name) with *kartā purakh* (creator person) orients the metaphysical One toward created phenomena – human and natural, generating a world-affirming theology. Importantly, the creator must not be cast as masculine for the Guru Granth Sahib maintains a gender-inclusive imaginary: "*āpe purakh āpe hī nārī* – the One is male; the One is female" (GGS: 1020); "in the male is the female, in the female male – *purakh mahi nāri nāri mahi purakhā*" (GGS: 879). Furthermore the reality of creation is validated throughout the Guru Granth Sahib: "the creator is truth; Its creation is true" (GGS: 294). There is no rupture between "the One" and "all things." Sikh religion espouses a panentheistic view that the creator person exists both within its vast and diverse creation, and also beyond all physical phenomena. The creator is related to the creation.[3]

This multiverse is the true house of the true One. The sole true creator is creating this entire cosmos with its planets, moon, sun, living beings in its own likeness: "True are Your realms, true the constellations, true Your worlds and true the shapes," extols Guru Nanak (GGS: 463). Nothing is false or illusionary for the one truth pervades each and every particle: "the earth is not false; water is not false" (GGS: 1240). Creation is not a completed process in the past tense but an active ongoing process taking place in the present and advancing into the future: "the creative creator is constantly creating, and beholding Its creation" (GGS: 7). We picture a mother watching over her child lovingly, being happy and reflecting upon him or her, and even being concerned about her or his future. The Gurus repeatedly say, "You bless us with Your love" (GGS: 1278). Divine love ripples across the Guru Granth Sahib.

We also get the image of the creator person as an artist who lovingly designs everyone and intimately sees Itself: "You designed each being, You recognize Yourself in each" (GGS: 1279). Everything in this multiverse mirrors that One. Humans are not Its only "image." The One takes on countless forms, informing every aspect of creation; nothing is devoid of the creator. The Sikh theological imaginary is an existential reality. Rather than an authoritarian controller or judge, the creator is a benevolent figure – a mother, a caretaker, a designer, an architect, an arranger. Interestingly, "the creator is also the enjoyer" (*ape kartā āpe bhugtā*) (GGS: 1035). Be it maternal creativity and/or magnificent artistry, all are palpably visible in this wondrous earth, this wondrous creation with its wondrous fire, water, species (GGS: 463–464).

Questions are also raised about origins: "What was the time, what was the hour? What was the date, what was the day? What was the season, what was the month, when creation came to be? (GGS: 4). Guru Nanak's questions echo questioning in the 129th hymn of the much earlier Indic scripture, the Rig Veda, as well as foreshadowing contemporary debates: When did it all come to be? How did everything form? He gives no answers. He mentions that even in his time scholars from diverse traditions were offering their own different answers but "if pandits knew the time it would be written in the Puranas, if qazis knew the hour it would be written in the Qur'an, no yogi knows the date or day, no one knows the month or season" (GGS: 4).

Not accepting any theories of creation, whether Hindu or Islamic, nor presuming any knowledge himself, the founder Sikh Guru incites his audience to think afresh about the vast temporal world that they all equally belong to. Devotees and scientists alike are welcome to the challenges that lie ahead in their quest. Sikh theology effectively shifts the attention from historical beliefs to future imaginings.[4]

*WITHOUT FEAR (*NIRBHAO)

The One's characteristic "without fear" (*nirbhao*) articulates the sovereignty of the creator. There is no other to threaten this One which is also without form (*nirankar*), and without hostility (*nirvairu*) (GGS: 596). As Guru Amar Das further qualifies, "the fearless One is always compassionate, taking care of each and all" (GGS: 27). These personality traits signify the One oriented toward Its creation courageously, wholesomely, full of love, compassion; subtly the verses elicit similar traits in the readers/listeners/reciters. In fact, people are exhorted repeatedly in the Guru Granth Sahib to remember the fearless One so all their own fears can dissipate. The daily evening prayer lyrically states, "Those who remember the fearless One, the fearless Divine, all their fears disappear" (GGS: 11). The guru even asks, "The fearless One is present with you, so what's there to fear?" (GGS: 206).

Sikhism maintains the distinction between the emotions of awe and fear. Awe is regarded positively because it evokes reverence and wonder for the infinite One and leads to knowledge and love not only for the infinite One but also for Its creation, animate and inanimate. Fear is crippling and inhibits access to the One, and produces social divisions. Only the egoistic person fears – fearing loss of wealth, health, status, or power. The dialectical pair *bhao* (fear) and *bhāo* (love, with a long "a") appears frequently in the Guru Granth Sahib. While fear is debilitating, love is empowering: the arteries have to be cleared of toxic fear (*bhao*) before nourishing love (*bhāo*) can circulate in the body so actions are performed for the collective good.

The biggest fear for humans is death. Since the body is mortal, humans across time and space have viewed it negatively as the opposite of immortal soul. Fully affirming the fluctuations of time, Guru Nanak courageously speaks about the unspeakable dread that can cripple every moment of life.[5] His mourning songs upend the traditional mourning rite that involved a group of women wailing at the house of the dead person for several days beating their breasts and thighs (a custom that lasted till quite recent times in the Punjab). Instead, the Sikh Guru invites people to come together but to mourn the emotional separation from the Divine, not physical death; to remember the Divine, not the dead; to rejoice in the splendor of this world and not lament any loss. His mourning songs squarely confront death so people may overcome the much-feared phenomenon: "Death would not have a bad name if only people knew what death is. . . Nanak, what's there to mourn for, Baba? This world is sheer magic" (GGS: 579). The attention is constantly drawn to the love for the all-inclusive One in this ever-changing world.

It is important to recognize that the fearless One in the Sikh theological imaginary evokes love and not anxiety or fear. That is why the lordly figure imposed in scriptural exegeses and translations is harmful. For example, even when there is no mention of such a figure in the original, Sirjanhar (creator) becomes "Creator Lord" in popular English versions. Psychologically the intimate love and care coming from Sirjanhar congeal, and distance and authority take over. Fear must be dispelled so we can make space for love. A positive energy, love for the singular fearless One, evokes heroic passion that reaches out as compassion from one body to the other to everything around.

WITHOUT HOSTILITY (NIRVAIRU)

Likewise, "without hostility" depicts the loving nature of the creator person as this One is "perpetually bestowing gifts" in the fifth Guru's definition (GGS: 287). It is important for humanity to realize the One does not harbor jealousy, anger, or any type of enmity (GGS: 1077); "by becoming hostile to the One without hostilities we set our home on fire" (GGS: 1415). Sikh Gurus witnessed the antagonism of their peers toward others simply because they belonged to another caste or religion or ethnicity or sex. The fear of the gaze, touch, and speech of a low-caste person or of a menstruating woman had been internalized by Indian society for centuries. Giving birth, a biologically natural mode of creation, was deemed dirty, with all sorts of lingering fears of pollution attached to it. The singular One, free of fear and hostility, is key to Sikh theology.

TIMELESS IMAGE (AKĀL MŪRAT)

"Timeless (*a* + *kāl*) image" underscores the infinity of the creator person. The One "cannot be molded into any form, cannot be shaped in any way," claims Guru Nanak early in the Japji (GGS: 1), so establishing an aniconic religion underscoring the vastness and infinity of the One who cannot be circumscribed in any which way.

BIRTHLESS (AJŪNĪ)

Birthless (*a* + *jūnī*) is an outright rejection of the doctrine of incarnation. The timeless One does not descend or appear in any body; It does not grow or die. This feature reiterates the timeless image that does not incarnate in any particular figure or form. Paradoxically, though, the formless One is each and every body and thing; the birthless One is copresent in the birth of every being in every single species: "You Yourself are born of the egg, from the womb, from sweat, from earth: You Yourself are all the continents and all the worlds" (GGS: 604). "Inside the womb flourishes the One," says Guru Nanak (GGS: 1026–1027). Sikh theology celebrates the plenitude of the One in every birth; indeed, the self-existent One exists in every atom of this multiverse.

*SELF-EXISTENT (*SAIBHAN)

The "timeless" "birthless" is "self-existent" (*svayyam-bhu*). In a lengthy 16-verse composition, Guru Nanak extols the transcendent One's total autonomy and self-existence: "When there was no celestial, terrestrial or netherworld, there was no time, no birth, no death. . . . There existed the 'One itself' (*eko soī*), 'enjoying while creating itself'" (GGS: 1035–1036). Sikh Gurus unanimously hymn the manifestation of the One even when nothing existed.

*GIFT OF THE GURU (*GURPRASÂD)

The finale of the *mūl mantar* returns to its beginning, the ever-presence of the infinite One. It recapitulates the sui generis attributes and thrusts the circle forward toward flesh-and-blood recipients, bonding the ontological Being with men and women who recognize the One in their particular historical, social, and personal reality. As noted before, the guru is a channel that brings the singular timeless birthless self-existent One to consciousness. The word *prasād* with its connotations "clearness," "gift," "sacred food" expresses the disclosure of the self-existent reality; what was banished from the consciousness is recovered in a palpable manner. This is sapiential knowledge uniquely experienced by every material body.

Although the language of the quintessential Sikh refrain asserts the One truth and identifies the creator Being as fearless (*nirbhao*), hate-free (*nirvairu*), timeless, and birthless, it is not the language of negative theology or negative dialectics of *neti neti*, typical of the Upanishadic tradition that Guru Nanak inherited. The *neti neti* process eliminates all objects of consciousness to realize the true nature of the formless (*nirguna*) Brahman, whereas the *mūl mantar*'s negations enhance the individual consciousness so it can hold on to the absolute, unconditioned self-existing nature of the singular reality each instant in every bit of everyday life. They compel audiences to emulate the fearless and friendly so they can bond with all the creatures of the timeless, birthless, self-existent creator person. The singular One's characteristic truth, devoid of fear and enmity, is much needed by global society today, full as it is of xenophobia, hatred, and suspicion of those we define as other.

THEOLOGICAL INTERSECTIONS: *HUKAM, LEKHĀ, QUDRAT, NADAR, KARAM,* AND *MUKTI*

Like most of Guru Granth Sahib diction, these recurrent terms are multivalent. However, they have been primarily associated by commentators with an all-powerful God, apart from this material world. It is important to go beneath their conceptual meaning to their existential meaning so that they are approached with the intention of the Guru Granth Sahib's authors – that is, receptively, relationally, interactively. These are not meant to be preconceived systematized doctrines. We regard them as energizing empowering intersections of the wondrous One with human praxis.

HUKAM *(CREATIVE DESIGN)*

From Arabic, *hukam* is routinely understood as "order," "divine ordinance," "command," "the sum total of all divinely instituted laws."[6] Such interpretations tend to connote the Divine as an authoritarian commander who evokes fear and surrender. The original exposition produces a different effect:

> In *hukam* all phenomena are formed,
> what *hukam* is no one can say.
> In *hukam* all life is formed, and honor received.
> *Hukam* makes heights and depths;
> *hukam* writes out joy and suffering.
> *Hukam* blesses some, others wander endlessly.
> All exist in *hukam*, nothing stands apart.
> *Nanak:* those who recognize [*bujhai*] *hukam*
> won't say "I" or "me" [*haumai*].[2]

Philosophy begins in wonder, and this introduction of *hukam* in the Japji evokes the ineffable artistic creativity, beauty, and magic of this multiverse. All material shapes and forms are being designed in *hukam*. Life is birthed in *hukam*; honor is given in *hukam*; everything good and bad is created in *hukam*; the circle of life and death is sundered in *hukam*. Rather than legalistic mechanisms such as "order" or "ordinance," a closer English equivalent for *hukam* would be "creative design." A design aspires for a balanced composition where positive elements and negative space are arranged so everything works together and fits together in a seamless whole, and *hukam* artistically creates and harmoniously sustains the physical, psychological, social, moral, and liberating patterns of this multiverse. As the 20th-century New Zealand historian of the Sikhs W.H. McLeod noted, "There is nothing random about *Hukam*. In Islam the divine Will, if not actually capricious is at least 'unpledged,' whereas the *Hukam* of Guru Nanak's usage is definitely pledged and dependable."[7]

Hukam in the Sikh context is juxtaposed with *haumai*, the toxic *I-me* (*hau*/I + *mai*/me), which obstructs the realization of the singular creative pattern of this diverse multiverse. Guru Nanak calls this dualistic ego a "false wall" (GGS: 1). As we read in the final line of the above passage, it is shattered by the realization (*bujhai*) of *hukam*, so there is no more a self-centered ego saying (*kahai*) "I-me" (*haumai*); there is only the experience of borderless unity. Clearly *hukam* is an emotive expansion of the individual self; rather than a complete surrender and submission to a monotheistic God, or fear of being judged by Him as habitually understood, *hukam* is a comforting snugness with the One and with fellow beings. Animate or inanimate, high or low, man or woman, all are embraced by *hukam* (*hukamai andar sabh ko*); together, interconnected, without hierarchies; nothing/nobody exists outside of this balanced, rhythmic pattern (*bāhar hukam nā koe*). The realization of our collective belonging promotes a harmonious kinship with the creator and Its vast creation; here is no chasm between the creator and the created, no divisive walls segregating created beings. *Hukam* espouses a recognition and appreciation of our pluriversal togetherness.

LEKHĀ *(THE WRITING)*

Lekhā (the writing) is also an all-embracing process and closely related with *hukam*. According to Guru Nanak, writing was the agent of creation at the very beginning of time. If *hukam* is the underpinning design, *lekhā* is the spatial and temporal expression of the spectacular diversity seen, heard, touched, tasted, and smelled. The Japji (stanza 16) describes the entire multiverse flowing out from a single pen stroke:

> The names of living beings, their varieties and colors,
> were all written in a single pen stroke.
> Were one to write this writ,
> what endless writ it would be.
> What power, beauty of form,
> how great a gift—how to assess it?
> This wide expanse from a single assent,
> from it a million rivers flowed forth.

The bountiful gift of the concrete writing is read in the incredible diversity of species and beings with different complexions; drawn by the same pen, the ontological design is visible everywhere.

The writing is not static. A dynamic movement toward the future, *lekhā* involves us humans. In fact, the deeds we are currently doing comprise its letters, vowels, and consonants. Words are identified with actions: "Good and evil are not mere words, the actions we do, get written and go with us: we reap only what we sow" (Japji stanza 20). The alliterative flow *kari kari karṇā* (actions we do) conveys the importance of doing actions, for each action bears its own result. We reap whatever choices we make, whatever moral values we live by. Daily actions are the words that get scripted on the forehead and go with people when they depart this world. There is total synchronicity between words and actions: "by words we name, by words we acclaim, by words we know and sing and praise; by words we write, speak, and perform, in words actions are written on our forehead, our blessed union proclaimed" (stanza 19). The actual words individuals write with their own sensibilities lead them to rebirth or free them from the cycle of transmigration to union with that infinite One.

QUDRAT *(CREATION, NATURE)*

The various cosmic phenomena are created by and in turn manifest the Divine, and so creation interacts with and rejoices in Its plenitude. The Arabic term *qudrat* is a disclosure of the universal reality:

> What we see is the One's *qudrat*.
> What we hear is the One's *qudrat*.
> *Qudrat* is at the core of happiness and fear.
> The skies, the nether regions and all that is visible is the One's *qudrat*.
> The Vedas, the Puranas, the Qur'an, indeed all thought is *qudrat*.
> Eating, drinking, dressing up is *qudrat*, so is all love *qudrat*!
>
> (GGS: 464)

To repeat: Sikh theology is inclusive theology for everything; everyone is the creation of the sole creator. All that is visible is the nature of that utterly invisible One, our first principle. It is the original force, the sole reality. Like *hukam* and *lekhā*, *qudrat* reveals a coherent and integrated system of the singular One proliferating existence. Physical matter including earth, skies, and nether regions; intellectual thought psychological states of joy, love, and fear; religious texts of Hindus and Muslims; practical activities like eating, drinking, and getting dressed make up Its body. In the passage above, syntactic, rhythmic, and semantic parallels relay the cosmos with all its doings as the nature of the sole reality. As such, there can be nothing beside the One and nothing outside of the One. The harmonious integration of all matter, thought, emotion, and action extends to people of different faiths. Indic and Abrahamic scriptures (*veda purāna katebā*) and all modes of thought and reflection (*sarab vīcār*) pulsate with the same One.

We must recognize the true One as the source and substance of this world, and enjoy Its beauty sustaining everybody. Guru Nanak laments the fact that people divide themselves by religious categories; boxed in, they are incapable of discerning their common denominator: "What can the poor Vedas and Kateb do when nobody recognizes the singular One?" (GGS: 1153). The whole of creation/nature is not something *from* the One but *of*

Itself, and so we must hear and see and taste and smell and touch every particle of the transcendent One.

NADAR *(LOVING LOOK)*

Derived from Arabic *nazar*, meaning "look" or "glance," *nadar* is a visual convergence of the finite person with the infinite One. However, it has been primarily translated as "grace." With its Christian undertones, "grace" does not convey the corporeal visuality central to Sikh religion. Seeing is an almost tactile sense, and *nadar* in the Sikh context is a tangible exchange between the creator and created beings, substantiating their relationality and intersubjectivity: "Just as the true One beholds so we become" (GGS: 66). Rather than a distant supreme arbitrator, *nadar* shows the transcendent One as a close, benevolent figure: "*kari kari vekhai nadar nihāl*" – "ever creating, It watches Its creation with Its loving look and delights" (Japji 37). There is a genuine reciprocity between actions of living beings and of the divine One. Transcendent eyes shower joy and freedom: "Says Nanak: seen by the loving look people are blissfully free" (Japji 38).

Seeing the One and being seen by that One express proximity and equality where subject-object duality dissolves; here is freedom from the cycle of birth and death, and the individual partakes the qualities of the birthless, timeless One.

In an era of alienation, the loving look from the transcendent One taking pleasure in its ongoing creativity endows the countless shapes and beings of this multiverse with significance. It also exudes warmth for fellow beings, and a sense of responsibility for the well-being of all.

KARAM *(ACTIONS)*

Karam refers to both actions and the fruit of actions, as the Sikh Gurus focus on the *how*, on the *doing*. In fact, individual identity is contingent on actions performed in social, political, commercial spheres: "Do not ask about caste or clan. . . . Caste and status are the actions we do," proclaims Guru Nanak categorically (GGS: 1330). Actions impact both mind and body: "Blind actions turn the mind blind, and the blind mind turns the body blind" (GGS: 1287).

Discarding conventional biologically stipulated actions that are determined by "caste" or gender or stage of life, Sikh religion upholds actions done for the collective good by five universally applicable virtues – truth (*sat*), contentment (*santokh*), morality (*dharam*), compassion (*daiā*), and tenacity (*dhīraj*). These five moral qualities are the effect of recognizing the all-inclusive One. There is no specification of any action or ritual or fasting or posture; doing ordinary everyday actions with the One in sight is the only Sikh prescription. By imagining the singular One, the practical infrastructure shifts from specific religious codes to fundamental human morality. For example, Guru Nanak exhorts people to go by the universal moral compass: "Violating another's rights is eating pork [for Muslims] and eating beef [for Hindus]. . . . Doing good actions is the only way to paradise" (GGS: 141).

Sikh theology is not fatalistic or deterministic. Humans have free will, and by the way they enact, they write out their destiny. While all actions are performed in the purview of the divine glance, people make their own moral choices as they follow the dictates of their individual volition. Regardless of family or gender or race or religion, everybody is endowed with the same five senses (*giān indriā*) – touching, hearing, smelling, seeing, and tasting. But how these are utilized differs from person to person, and their practice determines the two poles of the Sikh moral compass. Those who cultivate them into the five virtues are the guru-oriented ***gurmukh*s**; their antithesis are the self-centered ***manmukh*s** whose human faculties degenerate into vicious acts committed in lust (*kām*), anger (*krodh*), greed (*lobh*), attachment (*moh*), and pride (*ahankār*). These moral values apply to all of humanity. Existence is a privilege: "Life is precious like a diamond, but it can go for nought," cautions Guru Nanak (GGS: 156) Existence is treasured, and the existential goal is to be a virtuous agent, pursuing choices for world benefit.

Karam is paired with *nadar*: "actions bring us back in life, loving look gives us freedom" (Japji 4). Vicious actions jeopardize social cohesion and cosmic integration. They rob individuals of the underlying unity of humanity. Selfish ego asserts itself in opposition to others. Duality comes into play. Obsessed with I-me (*haumai*), the individual is blind to the singular One. There is no visual reciprocity between the self and the Divine, and so these people remain bound in the cycle of transmigration. In contrast, actions performed with the One in sight are reciprocated with the loving look, fusing the individual with the infinite One. By their own doing people escape finite confinements imposed by the circle of "coming and going – *āvā gavan*," to use the Guru's phrase for reincarnation. Humans are endowed with agency: they can inscribe their writing on their foreheads that either brings them back to birth or unites them with the timeless birthless One.

MUKTI *(FREEDOM)*

Mukti (*moksha* in older Indic thought) is liberation, a free, blissful state of union with the ultimate One. When finite beings feel the vast, timeless truth, their dualistic selfish confinements shatter, so they live truthfully, without any fear or hostility. Absorbing the all-inclusive One, all divisive and oppressive "isms" of racism, sexism, classism, religious fanaticism disperse, so people free themselves from the cycle of rebirth; "they never again return to the womb of reincarnation," says Guru Nanak (GGS: 1040). The doctrine of transmigration, which is central to Hindus, Buddhists, and Jains, is brought up in the Guru Granth Sahib, but it does not play as vital a role. In the Sikh religion, *mukti* is not a happening after death, nor is it a turning away from the social, economic, and pleasures of this world; essential to daily existence, *mukti* is integrated into social morality (*dharam*), economic prosperity (*artha*), and pleasures of life (*kama*). Guru Arjan praises the singular creator for instantly gifting these four human aspirations (GGS: 816). Communal interactions are the impetus for personal joy and success, for ultimate freedom and bliss, and *mukti* is posited as a lifestyle conducted in the company of good people (GGS: 407). "Those who hold the true One in their heart, their vision is true, their conduct is true, their speech is true, their form is true, and they merge with truth" (GGS: 283). *Mukti* is a joyous existential modality here in this world, which continues in the hereafter. In brief, it is a mode of being with Being. The focus of the Sikh religion is not on heaven and hell beyond death but on living fruitfully engaged with fellow beings, ever alive to the touch of the one formless truth – *ikkoankār sat nām*.

THEOLOGICAL QUEST: THE FIVE *KHAṆḌS*

The celebration of the divine One named truth in the Japji prologue culminates with an ever-widening existential journey to the realm of that One (*sac khanḍ*, literally "realm of truth"). With maps and charts drafted entirely on the longitudes and latitudes of planet earth, readers and reciters voyage across the five spheres (*khanḍs*) – *dharam* (morality), *gīān* (knowledge), *saram* (beauty), *karam* (actions), and *sac* (truth). This journey is not an ascension into some higher region beyond life and the world; rather, it is a quest to pull the infinite One into the basics of daily life. Human subjectivity engages meaningfully in these five spheres and, in turn, provides an understanding of Sikh ontic, epistemological, aesthetic, ethical, and liberating currents.

ONTIC: *DHARAM* (MORALITY)

The pan-Indian term *dharam* (or *dharma*) is widely used for religion, virtue, duty, propriety, morality, cosmic order, law, and more. In the Sikh religion, *dharam* (morality) is grounded in our social equality as opposed to the conventional Indic *varna-ashrama-dharma* social categories (*varna*) of Brahmins, Kshatriyas, Vaishyas, and Shudras. It is also based on lifelong involvement and responsibility, as opposed to the older Indic model of different successive modes of conduct based on the stages of life (*āshrama*) – *brahmacarin, grahastha, vānaprastha*, and *sanyāsin* (i.e., the stages that are marked respectively by the absence of sex and marriage, then the phase of family life, and thereafter, the periods of withdrawing from social responsibilities and finally of total renunciation of the world). There are no stipulations for any gender differences or bias either, for there is no separate *stridharma* (woman's *dharma*) as in traditional Indic codes: "There is only one Dharam – *eko dharam*," declares Guru Nanak (GGS: 1188). "Be they Kshatriyas, Brahmins, Shudras or Vaishyas, everybody shares the same mandate," reiterates Guru Arjan (GGS: 747). *Dharam* in Sikh religiosity constitutes the very being of a person – their personal and social morality, their temporality, their materiality, their divinity. The Sikh Gurus identify *dharam* with the earth – "the earth is Dharam" (GGS: 302), and "the body itself in its entirety is

Dharam, it holds the true One's light" (GGS: 309). *Dharam* is our physical and spiritual reality.

The Japji describes *dharam* as an expansive stage with the earth set amid numerous planets. At the starting point of the existential journey, the reader's attention is drawn to their temporal, geographical, social, and cosmic ontology:

> Amid nights and seasons, dates and days,
> air, water, fire, and netherworlds,
> in their middle is the earth, the place of righteous action.
> In its midst beings and lifestyles of all colors.
>
> (GGS: 7)

To carry out moral responsibilities, we first need to know our concrete historical context. The subtle distinction between *vār* (the days of the week) and *thitī* (the dates of the lunar month) urges each reader to think about the precise time of their situatedness so they can make the most of that instant here and now. Simultaneously billions of years behind come to mind as do billions yet to come. Daily calendars with their narrow standards of measurement acquire a much larger vista. The onset of the journey ignites respect and appreciation for temporal movements, compelling humans to take up their responsibility in maintaining the intricate web of relationships. Time is an essential element of life, and the intersection of personal and cosmic time challenges readers to change their selfish attitudes and behavior. What do we learn from the past? How could we neglect future generations? How could we destroy our ecosystem?

Humans are also made aware of their spatiality, their materiality. What are we made of? We are basically elements – air (*pavaṇ*), water (*pāṇī*), fire (*agni*), earth (*pātāl*), and their compounds. Humans are not set apart from other species, nor is the living set apart from the inanimate. Rather than an alienated anthropomorphic attitude, individual existence is understood to be woven into the wider cosmic environment. In Sikh theology all beings share the same elemental makeup, they share the singular source, and are a part of the reality of the diverse chemical, biological, and material shapes and forms.

Importantly, though, human and cosmic oneness and equality does *not* denote uniformity. The sphere of *dharam* as we discussed is a rejoicing in the diversity of planet earth: "In its midst are beings and lifestyles of all hues, with endless names and countless forms." No two bodies are alike. Against homogenization Guru Nanak celebrates diversity in all its manifestations. In his lifetime the founder Guru traveled widely, meeting people from different religious backgrounds, and he enjoined living authentically, matching one's inner values with one's outward behavior. His respect for the diversity of human experience is an important lesson for modern society: unless we appreciate diversity, we cannot coexist harmoniously with others who happen to be different from us. The appreciation of kinship comes with the realization that all particularities palpitate with the same One – "all species and languages come together in You" (GGS: 1021).

Only the realization that we belong to a vast temporal and spatial horizon full of diverse fellow beings motivates ethical and purposeful actions: "The earth is placed for righteous action." The true creator is constantly present in our interactions, for each action we do is reflected on by that One. Another Guru Granth Sahib verse states, "For the sake of good people the earth is embellished" (GGS: 941). The earth is beautiful, and humans are created to do good, so we must all work together to maintain the beauty and splendor of the earth, not only for ourselves but also for our future generations.

EPISTEMOLOGY: *GĪĀN* (KNOWLEDGE)

The second existential stage pertains to "knowledge." *Gīān khanḍ* (GGS: 7) showcases a panoramic spectacle of countless varieties of atmosphere, water, and fire (*kete pavaṇ pāṇī vaisantar*), countless inhabited planets like mother earth (*ketīā karam bhumī*), countless mountains (*mer kete*), countless moons (*kete cand*), suns (*sūr*), and constellations (*manḍal des*). Audiences witness innumerable gods and goddesses, teachers and masters: "How many Krishnas and Shivas, how many Brahmas were created in millions of forms . . . countless siddhas, buddhas, nathas, and so many, many goddesses." Figures of Indian religious history and religious systems like the Vaishnavites, Shaivites, Buddhists, and Naths are all included. But knowing this panorama is not enough. How to grasp these countless entities? How to appreciate their vast diversity? How to make the vast knowledge a part of the personal self? How to feel this endless multiverse? Living out a diverse spectrum of knowledge is critical to Sikh epistemology.

AESTHETIC: *SARAM* (BEAUTY)

Saram (beauty), the sphere of aesthetics, is the answer (GGS: 8). Aesthetics (in contrast to anesthesia) is the heightening of sensibilities, a convergence of the sensuous, cognitive, artistic, and spiritual dimensions. Expanded knowledge burns away myopic stereotypes and prejudices, so artistic faculties are fired up. According to Guru Nanak, the beauty of Saram Khanḍ cannot be adequately described (*kathīā na jāhī*) and the designs created here are beyond parallel (*anūp*). It is in this sphere that consciousness (*surat*), wisdom (*mat*), mind (*man*), and power of discrimination (*buddhī*) are sharpened (*ghaṛiaī*). However blunt mental, psychological, intellectual, and reasoning faculties may be, they are developed and chiseled in this realm of art and beauty. Conceptual knowledge is not enough, aesthetic experience is vital to the absorption of the vast geometry of the world outlined in the previous realm of knowledge. Bodily feelings, and emotions make meaning possible as they provide experiential understanding. "Only the one who enjoys the scent knows the flower," said Guru Nanak (GGS: 725).

The honing that takes place in Saram Khanḍ leads to mystical and divine knowledge: "Here consciousness is sharpened to that of gods and mystics" (last line of the stanza). All thinking is spurred by an aesthetic sensibility which so refines human faculties that the individual experiences union with the infinite plurality of subjects acknowledged in Gīān Khanḍ. All distance and divisions between what is to be known and the knower, what is seen and the seer, are erased. It is at this threshold that the agents step up to the sphere of actions, Karam Khanḍ (stanza 37), where they join "mighty warriors and heroes" (*tithai jodh mahābal sūr*), and inhabitants who perform "joyous actions" (*karahi anandu*).

ETHICS: *KARAM* (ACTIONS)

In this realm of actions (*karam*) we find beautiful heroes, both male and female, and devotees from different traditions working energetically. These ethical exemplars, including the cherished Sita (the heroine of the Ramayana) and her companions, are aesthetically refined. These aesthetes are heroically charged with the One and enjoy working for the common good. They embody the fearless and nonhostile nature of the One articulated in the *mūl mantar*. That they embrace the infinite One in their heart is repeated three times in the short Japji stanza. In the sphere of action (*karam*) embodied beings live out truth (*sac*). Not a conceptual category, ontological truth is aesthetically enhanced praxis.

ULTIMATE LIBERATION: *SAC* (TRUTH)

From the wide-ranging, inclusive, and egalitarian realm of actions, voyagers make it to the "realm of truth where lives the formless One – *sac khanḍ vasai nirankār*" (stanza 37). The fifth and final sphere, that of truth (*sac khanḍ*), expresses Guru Nanak's ultimate goal: union with the One named truth. Compositionally set together in the same stanza (37), the spheres of action (*karam*) and truth (*sac*) synchronize worldly actions with transcendent truth. Here are no boundaries, no demarcations of any sort as the dwelling place never ends – "here are continents, constellations, and universes, their counting never ending, never . . . " This borderless sphere where the formless One (*nirankār*) dwells is no different from the world upon worlds of shapes and forms (*loa loa akār*). A fusion of the material and transcendent horizons, the limitless *sac khanḍ* is the climax of the Sikh theological quest. It is the experience of total liberation (*mukti* or *moksha*).

In *sac khanḍ* the self and the One become a unity, an ineffable juncture wherein the seeing by the individual becomes the seeing by the transcendent. In the concluding verse of stanza 37, the One "watches, rejoices, and reflects on creation, says Nanak, to describe this is as hard as iron." A continuous and unconditional love pours forth from that One, and in this ultimate liberation, there is no sense of conflict between the finite subject and the infinite Divine. To describe their union is hard – "as hard as iron" is Guru Nanak's simile.

Evidently this world and the beyond are no different. Planet earth provides us with our existential reality (*dharam*) so we can expand our knowledge (*gīān*), refine ourselves aesthetically (*saram*), engage in heroic actions (*karam*), and live with and in truth (*sac*). To sum it all up, Sikh theology articulates a vibrant coexistence with the timeless, birthless, fearless, nonhostile, self-manifest singular creator that we all share, the One named truth.

NOTES

1 Paul Ricoeur, "Philosophy and Religious Language," *Journal of Religion* 54, no. 1 (1974): 73.
2 Nikky-Guninder Kaur Singh, *The Feminine Principle in the Sikh Vision of the Transcendent* (Cambridge: Cambridge University Press, 1993).
3 Mary Potter Engel, Carol P. Christ, M. Shawn Copeland, Wonhee Anne Joh, Julie B. Miller, Nancy Pineda-Madrid, and Masako Kuroki, "Roundtable Discussion: Mysticism and Feminist Spirituality," *Journal of Feminist Studies in Religion* 24, no. 2 (2008): 164–167.
4 Nikky-Guninder Kaur Singh, *Guru Nanak's Transcendent Aesthetics* (Cambridge: Cambridge University Press, 2024).
5 Harbans Singh, *Guru Nanak and Origins of the Sikh Faith* (Bombay: Asia Publishing House, 1969), 214.
6 W.H. McLeod, *Guru Nanak and the Sikh Religion* (Oxford: Clarendon Press, 1968), 203. See also G.S. Talib, *Japji: The Immortal Prayer-Chant* (New Delhi: Munshiram Manoharlal, 1977), 89–91.
7 W.H. McLeod, *Guru Nanak and the Sikh Religion*, 201.

REFERENCES AND FURTHER READING

McLeod, W.H. *Guru Nanak and the Sikh Religion*. Oxford: Clarendon Press, 1968.

Shackle, Christopher, and Arvind-pal Singh Mandair. *Teachings of the Sikh Gurus: Selections from the Sikh Scriptures*. London: Routledge, 2005.

Singh, Nikky-Guninder. *First Sikh: Life and Legacy of Guru Nanak*. New Delhi: Penguin Random House, 2019.

Singh, Nikky-Guninder Kaur. *Poems from the Sikh Sacred Tradition*. Cambridge, MA: Harvard University Press, 2023.

Singh, Nikky-Guninder Kaur. *The Feminine Principle in the Sikh Vision of the Transcendent*. Cambridge: Cambridge University Press, 1993.

Singh, Nikky-Guninder Kaur. *Guru Nanak's Transcendent Aesthetics*. Cambridge: Cambridge University Press, 2025.

Talib, G.S. *Japji: The Immortal Prayer-Chant*. New Delhi: Munshiram Manoharlal, 1977.

4

PRACTICES

Sikh greetings welcome the Divine, as when Sikhs greet or part from each other, they tend to join their hands and say *Sat Sri Akal* (Truth is timeless). Their frequent exclamation "*Waheguru*" echoes the wonders of the all-inclusive wondrous One celebrated across Sikh scripture. The Sikh Gurus sought to transform society and the Guru Granth Sahib is the source for practitioners to free themselves from earlier codes and invest their lifestyle with the spiritual energy of the One, *ikkoankār*.

SIKH SACRED TEXT: THE GURU GRANTH SAHIB

For most Sikhs the Guru Granth Sahib is the center of their life. Whether privately at home or in the public space of the gurdwara (literally "door to the Guru"), the volume is venerated. It is draped in silks and brocades (called *rumālā*), placed on quilted mats, and supported by cushions. A protective canopy hangs above it, and an attendant waves over it a *chaurī* (a hand fan, often made of white yak tail hair). Such cultural symbols express the sovereign status of the scriptural Guru. Men, women, and children remove their shoes and cover their heads before coming into its presence. Its 1,430 pages (the standard number in single-volume printed editions) celebrate the Divine as the one universal matrix. The Guru Granth Sahib, a body of exalted poetry, remains in touch with everyday reality. Without stipulating rules and regulations, it serves as a guide to practical, moral, and spiritual life. This sole sovereign of the Sikhs presides at daily worship and all ceremonies, and rites of passage.

DOI: 10.4324/9781003359210-4

Devotion entails *mathā ṭeknā* to the Guru Granth Sahib and *darshan karnā* (seeing it and so receiving its blessing). Devotees perform *mathā teknā* by going down on both their knees in reverent submission and bowing low till their forehead (*mathā*) touches the floor in front of the sacred text. Many offer money; some offer flowers. *Darshan* is an originally Hindu religious practice of seeing, and being seen by, the Divine. For Sikhs, catching a glimpse of their text, listening to it or reading it, singing, or just sitting in its presence constitute "taking *darshan*."

Daily the Guru Granth Sahib is opened at dawn and draped in decorative *rumālā*s. The morning ceremony is *prakāsh*, "making the light manifest." It is a ritual enactment of the Guru being enthroned and ready to receive the public and radiate its luminosity. The *hukamnāmā* (instruction) or *vāk* (reading) of the day is obtained by reverently opening the Guru Granth Sahib at random, and reading the passage on the top of the left-hand page, which is understood as the message for the day. The *hukamnāmā/vāk* at a gurdwara is displayed on a board so that visitors throughout the day can read and interpret it for themselves. For any major decision or undertaking, whether individual or collective – and in making everyday choices – Sikhs may solicit scriptural guidance by taking a *hukamnāmā/vāk*. Nowadays, Sikhs worldwide can electronically access the daily message from the Golden Temple. With the televising of its morning and evening ceremonies, Sikh devotees can participate in their tradition in a new way. The televising is also impacting public worship elsewhere, as more and more gurdwaras try to follow the standard routine at the Golden Temple.

In the evening the Guru Granth Sahib is ceremonially closed. This closing ritual is called *sukhāsan*, the position (*āsan*) of rest or comfort (*sukh*) for the night. The *sukhāsan* parallels the morning *prakāsh*, and the two create the daily framework for congregations to attend to their sacred volume. In gurdwaras, these ceremonies are more elaborate than at home. In the Golden Temple, the Guru Granth Sahib is carried in a gold and silver palanquin (*palkī*) from the Harmandar and along the causeway to the Akāl Takht for its nightly rest. Worshippers pay homage by shouldering the palanquin. The melody of the evening Arati hymn brings harmony and joy as its imagery evokes the Indic way of worshipping by circling a tray holding lamps, incense, flowers, and fruit around a devotee's favorite deities. In Guru Nanak's Arati hymn, the ritual is metamorphosed into a cosmic choreography of the planets: the sky being the tray (*thāl*) on which the sun, moon, and stars perform *āratī* around the infinite One.

The Gurus' poetry has been institutionalized into Sikh practices as it is read for all rites of passage, for any family celebration – of a new house, a new job, birthdays, or engagements, and also in times of sickness and death. Often the reading at these events is *akhanḍ* (unbroken) a 48-hour, nonstop reading, during which readers take turns.[1] Any Sikh, male or female, who can read Gurmukhi script may read the Guru Granth Sahib. The reading ends with *bhog* (literally meaning "pleasure") which involves reading the concluding pages and the distribution of the warm, sweet, aromatic *kaṛāh prashād*.

Kaṛāh prashād is made of equal portions of butter, flour, sugar, and water, vigorously stirred on a stove so that it remains moist and sticky. During its preparation men and women keep their heads covered, their feet bare, and recite the Gurus' verses. When ready, it is put in a large dish and placed right next to the Guru Granth Sahib. As the finale of worship, it is distributed to the entire congregation, who receive it in cupped palms – with both hands joined together.

SIKH SACRED SPACE: GURDWARA

The Sikh place of public worship is called a gurdwara – that is, a doorway or threshold (*dwara*) to spiritual awakening (*guru*). Historical gurdwaras were constructed to mark important events in Sikh history, and community gurdwaras are built to meet local religious and social needs. A typical gurdwara is open all day, with devotees coming and going whenever they wish. Religious activity consists of seeing the Guru Granth Sahib or listening to it being read or interpreted or sung, and this can be done either individually or with the rest of the congregation. Most gurdwaras serve community meals (*langar*) on a regular basis, and some have room for pilgrims to stay. Gurdwaras are more than places of worship as they provide assistance, food, shelter, and fellowship. The Guru Granth Sahib is the focal point to which everyone has equal access. There are no three-dimensional images in the gurdwara. Parts of the building often display pictures of the Gurus, of Harmandar Sahib, and of traumatic events in Sikh history.

Besides the Harmandar, there are five popular pilgrimage sites, called the five ***takht*s** (seats or thrones). The Akāl Takht, facing the Golden Temple in Amritsar, is regarded as the supreme seat of religious and temporal authority. The other four are associated with the tenth Guru: Patna Sahib in Bihar, his birthplace; Keshgarh Sahib, in Anandpur (Punjab), where he created the Khalsa; and Hazur Sahib in Nanded, Maharashtra, where he breathed his last. Damdama Sahib, near Bhatinda in Punjab, where the Guru took rest, later became a center of Sikh learning.

Although pilgrimage is not a religious requirement, many Sikhs try to visit the five *takht*s at least once in their lifetime.

Other places marking the birth of the Gurus or the sites they visited are also venerated. Even if they cannot go in person, devotees send money for scriptural readings, for the community kitchen, for the general upkeep of the shrine, and for gifts such as the *rumālā*s.

FIVE DAILY PRAYERS

The daily spiritual routine (*nitnem*) consists of recitation or reading (*pāṭh*) of hymns from the Guru Granth Sahib. Some devotees recite the five daily prayers from memory, some read them, others listen to their live or recorded recitations. Every morning and evening Sikh sacred spaces and homes (and even cars and trucks) resonate with the melodious sounds of their daily hymns. Children hear them from their parents as they carry out their daily chores of cooking, combing hair, watering plants. The Japji, Jāp, Swayyai, Rahiras, and Kirtan Sohila constitute the daily repertoire. There is no rigid timing for any of the five. However, the Japji, Jāp, and Swayyai are recited in the morning; the Rahiras and, later, the Kirtan Sohila in the evening.

As we have seen, Guru Nanak's Japji presents Sikhs' fundamental philosophical and ethical beliefs. It is recited at dawn when the mind is fresh and the atmosphere is serene. Described in the Japji as the ambrosial time, the three hours before dawn are generally considered most conducive to grasping the divine word and having a deeper communion with the One.

Jāp and Swayyai are the compositions of the tenth Guru. They are from Guru Gobind Singh's Dasam Granth. Although the Guru Granth Sahib forms the center of Sikh worship, Sikhs also esteem the tenth Guru's poetry, and so the Jāp and the Swayyai are part of their daily prayers. Jāp, a breathtaking profusion of divine attributes, ends with couplet 199, so signifying that there is no culmination.

Swayyai are quatrains. The ten Swayyai included in the daily prayers underscore devotion as the essence of religious practice. Rejecting all forms of external worship, they cast Guru Nanak's message of internal love in undulating rhythm. They are also recited during the administration of *amrit*, the Khalsa's initiation ceremony.

Rahiras, the early evening prayer, comprises hymns by Guru Nanak, Guru Amar Das, Guru Ram Das, and Guru Arjan, and Guru Gobind Singh's Chaupai Benti (supplication in quatrains). The Rahiras concludes with the first five stanzas and the final stanza of Guru Amar Das's Anand (Bliss). Sikhs recite Rahiras during the reflective period of dusk. Through the Rahiras, the Sikhs pay homage to the transcendent One, they seek the singular creator's protection and succor, and express their joy upon hearing the melodious Word in their deepest self.

Kirtan Sohila, meaning the hymn of praise, is the finale to the evening routine and is also recited at cremation ceremonies, so linking the end of life with the end of the day. Kirtan Sohila consists of five hymns, the first three by Guru Nanak, followed by one each from Guru Ram Das and Guru Arjan. The first hymn visualizes the union of the individual self with the Divine. The second underscores the singularity of the Divine, despite the endless diversity of scriptures, teachers, and philosophies. The third is Guru Nanak's Arati, imaging the entire cosmos harmoniously worshipping the One. Its fourth hymn (by Guru Ram Das) explains the import of the divine name which annuls suffering and transmigration. The fifth hymn (by Guru Arjan) celebrates life on earth, an opportunity for everybody to serve others and win divine merit. The transcendent mystery is revealed within the body, and so the enlightened enjoy the blissful freedom of immortality.

Ardās (from the Persian word *arz-dasht*, a written petition) is recited morning and evening, led by a leading member of the congregation. The entire gathering stands facing the Guru Granth Sahib with hands folded and heads bowed. The congregation joins in at intervals, exclaiming "Waheguru!" ("Wonderful Guru!"). Ardās always includes remembering the divine One, the ten Gurus, their merging with the Guru Granth Sahib, and events of Sikh heroism, devotion, and martyrdom. Toward the end, a blessing is invoked for the specific purpose for which the congregation gathered. Ardās ends by praying for a buoyant spirit (*caṛdī kalā*) and the prosperity of all beings (*sarbat dā bhalā*).

Sukhmani (by Guru Arjan) is not part of the daily routine, but this relatively long composition, extolling the divine name, is frequently recited. *Sukh* means "peace" and *manī* is either "pearl" or "mind" (from the word *manu*), so the title can be translated as "Pearl of Peace" or "Peace of Mind." When read in groups, several copies of the hymn are made available. Someone begins to read out a section, and anyone who wishes may join at the end to lead in the reading of the next section. The final couplets in each segment are read by the group in unison.

KEY SIKH INSTITUTIONS

There are four key Sikh institutions: *sangat, kīrtan, langar*, and *sevā*. These are essentially democratic, emancipatory, and empathy-generating practices.

SANGAT

Worldwide, any Sikh gathering or local community comprises a *sangat*. *Sangat* praxis underscores the importance of togetherness and equality. Religiosity involves comradeship (not isolation and renunciation), so nurturing active and fruitful engagement with others. According to a popular Sikh saying, "One disciple is a single Sikh, two form a holy association, but where five are present, there is the divine Itself." Being together generates a feeling of kinship of the sort that the cultural anthropologist Victor Turner categorizes as "spontaneous" or "existential *communitas*."[2] This internal connection with others is vital to the Sikh way of life: "There is no satisfaction without the company of the good" (GGS: 20); "It is only in the company of the good that we taste divine elixir" (GGS: 598); and "So glorious is true company that we recognize reality, we get to know true being" (GGS: 1026).

The 19th-century French sociologist Émile Durkheim's anthropological reflections further illuminate *sangat* dynamics: "When they are once come together, a sort of electricity is formed by their collecting which quickly transports them to an extraordinary degree of exaltation. Every sentiment expressed finds a place without resistance in all the minds, which are very open to outside impressions; each re-echoes the others and is re-echoed by the others."[3] In the Guru Granth Sahib good friends are compared with a perfume container which we must open to breathe in the scent: "With our body bound to theirs, our thoughts fused" (GGS: 765). True companionship transforms the state of imperfect existence into one of spiritual perfection: "Just as iron rubbed against the philosopher's stone turns into gold, so does dark ignorance transform into brilliant light in the company of the good" (GGS: 505). Affirming marriage, family, and society, *sangat* promotes spiritual realization in the company of fellow beings.

In Sikh congregations, members sit together on the floor (though men and women usually sit on different sides) all facing the sacred volume and singing hymns, listening to expositions of the sacred text, reciting verses, and praying. The shared experience transcending sociostructural positioning was the hallmark of Guru Nanak's liberative philosophy. The aspiration (if not always the reality) is to relate empathetically across sects, races, nations, classes, and cliques. But how do we "recognize (*pachānai*) ourself (*āp*) in every (*sarab*) being (*jīā*)"? Guru Nanak "saw no stranger" because he recognized physical sensibilities common to everybody.[4] His final successor, Guru Gobind Singh, reiterates, "Different vestures from different countries may make us appear different, we have the same eyes, the same ears, the same body, the same voice" (Akāl Ustati: 86). The corporeal body derives its energy from the infinite One within: "There is a light in all and that light is that One," goes Guru Nanak's maxim recited daily in the evening Arati which started with the Kartarpur community and continues today.

Foremost Sikh historian Bhai Gurdas, the contemporary of several Gurus, describes the revolutionary spirit unleashed by the first Sikh Guru: "He turned the four castes into the same one"; "the rich and the poor have become equal"; "Ganga is made to flow in the opposite direction!" (Var I:38). In lengthy passages Bhai Gurdas conveys the radical social and religious transformation produced by Nanakian *sangat*: "Just as a needle sews materials ripped asunder, he brings harmony to the torn and conflicting groups of Hindus and Muslims" (Var 33:4). Divine praise, generosity, and a routine of cleanliness (inner and outer) became the paradigmatic mode of existence (Var 1:23).

Closer to our times, we note that *sangat* bears a striking affinity to Martin Luther King Jr.'s "Beloved Community" and Desmond Tutu's "*ubuntu*" as their substratum is the equality, interconnectedness, and enhancement of humanity. In the physical proximity of good people, goodness is contagious: *sangat* is a touchstone against all sorts of segregation and discrimination. The first *sangat* started by Guru Nanak may have been small, but its ecumenical momentum now inspires a global *sangat*.

KĪRTAN

Sikhs' central devotional practice has always been *kīrtan*, "singing, listening, and nurturing love" (*gāviai, suniai, mani rakhiai bhāu*), as stated by Guru Nanak in his Japji. Song was Guru Nanak's medium of divine praise. Bhai Gurdas and other historical sources tell us that the Guru traveled extensively with his childhood companion Mardana, who played the rabab while Nanak extolled the transcendent Being: thus the Guru Granth Sahib's musical infrastructure originates in that intersection of human and divine, Sikh and Muslim, vocal and instrumental. Later the Kartarpur community gathered around Guru Nanak to sing, recite, and hear his melodies of divine love. In Bhai Gurdas's poetic testimony, "Sodar and Arati were sung in the evening, Jap was recited in the morning" (Var 1:38) and "each and every home resounds with Baba's songs; music of drums and rabāb fills the air" (Var 24:4). Artistically he conveys the infectious effect: "like the fragrant sandalwood makes all vegetation fragrant." Guru Nanak's successors built on his musical praxis. As outlined earlier, most compositions in the Guru Granth Sahib are framed in 31 rāga sections belonging to the traditional South Asian musical measures, and as we will see in chapter 7, the musical past looks set to enrich the future of *kīrtan*.

According to Guru Arjan, the compiler-editor of the Guru Granth Sahib, "*tahā baikunṭh jah kīrtan terā*" – "it is paradise where Your *kīrtan* is performed" (GGS: 749). Guru Arjan uses the pronoun "*terā*" (Your) with reference to the universal Patron who initially employed Nanak. Upholding Guru Nanak's pluralistic aesthetics, Guru Arjan gathered together spiritual lyrics spanning religions, centuries, geographical regions, ethnicities, cultures, languages, castes, classes, and musical measures. So Sikh sacred spaces, homes, shops, vehicles are infused with melodies not only of the Sikh Gurus but also of Muslim Sheikh Farid, Hindu Namdev, bards Satta and Balvand, and many more.

LANGAR

Like *kīrtan*, the Sikh *langar* (community meal) goes back to people who gathered around Nanak. The earliest memories of Guru Nanak register the importance he gave to food and its consumption in the company of others. A narrative from the *B-40 Janamsākhī* text recounts his discourse with a group of ascetics practicing severe austerities up in the Himalayas. The Guru beholds them fasting and dipping their bodies into icy cold water where some even die. He then points them to a lukewarm lake to bathe in, and with his cupped hands that can hold pounds of rice, ghee, and sugar, he feeds the famished ascetics.[5] As other *janamsākhī*s narrate, when his father gave the young Nanak money to start a business, he chose to feed hungry ascetics instead. When he worked as the governor's storekeeper, he would, according to Sikh tradition, give food to those in need. According to another *B-40* narrative, he ensured that the *langar* be served twice daily and that it includes items that people would savor (*bhuncaï*).[6] This sensuous verb appears too in the epilogue of the Guru Granth Sahib composed by Guru Arjan (GGS: 1429) for savoring the scriptural contents. Food and knowledge maintain a symbiotic relationship, and the scriptural reference to Mata Khivi's cooking (see chapter 1) suggests that the Sikh institution of *langar* began early in the evolution of Sikhism.

A desegregating commensality is the keynote of *langar*. Preparing meals and eating together across caste, class, religion, and gender lines was a radical rupture of normative societal hierarchies. Like *kīrtan*, the practice of *langar*, has evolved in unprecedented ways. Volunteers in gurdwaras in India and abroad prepare *langar* and serve it to people irrespective of religious or social divisions. In the *langar* hall of the Golden Temple in Amritsar, about 80,000 visitors daily eat meals prepared by enthusiastic volunteers. At weekends and on festivals, almost twice as many are served in what the *New York Times* called the "world's largest free eatery."[7] Similarly, Guru Singh Sabha Gurdwara in Southall, United Kingdom, serves thousands of meals. Everybody partakes – in most cases sitting on the floor and so expressing their equality.[8] During COVID-19, *langars* in New York City supplied basmati rice, lentils, vegetable dishes to hospital workers, the homeless, and anyone needing a hot meal. In Delhi, even an "oxygen *langar*" was set up. Then, during the farmers' protest movement in 2020–2021 (see chapter 7), impromptu kitchens on roadsides sprang up near Delhi to feed the masses: men and women cooked in open-air kitchens as truckloads of vegetables, flour, oil, and milk arrived daily from villages and towns – along with sacks of almonds supplied by California-based Sikhs. *Langar* has entered academia, too: the University of Denver has developed a full credit course incorporating *langar* as the basis for building community.[9]

Why is *langar* placed center stage in Sikh religiosity? Its significance is traced to Guru Nanak's embodied revelation when he consumed food and drink given to him by the all-inclusive Divine.[10] The community meal became the mode to demolish religiously, socially, and psychologically ossified hierarchical structures that robbed people of respect for their body and identity. Rules of purity and pollution – what was taken inside the body and with whom – had led to segregation based on caste and religion. Guru Nanak sharply criticized the stringent food norms upheld by his hegemonic Brahmanical society. No substance was polluted in itself: the categories of purity and pollution were human concoctions: "The mind's pollution is greed, the tongue's is lies, the pollution of the eyes is to covet another's wife, wealth, beauty; the ears' pollution is to hear malice and thrive on mistrust" (GGS: 472). Five hundred years ago the Sikh Guru had recognized that the social infrastructure of caste was the artificial, arbitrary graded ranking of human value analyzed recently by Isabel Wilkerson in *Caste: The Origins of Our Discontents.*[11]

Langar affirms familyhood among people and evokes respect for ingredients: "Grain is holy, water is holy, fire is holy, salt too, and by adding ghee, the fifth, our food is purer still," declares the Guru Granth Sahib (GGS: 473). *Langar* elicits respect for the water, seasons, bees, and the environment that enable production of food, respect for the acts of cooking and eating, respect for the bodies we cook and dine with, and ultimately respect for our daily lives. A widespread narrative in public memory highlights the Sikh stress on food ethics: when Nanak squeezed fancy bread from the wealthy exploitative Malik Bhago, blood spattered; when he squeezed a plain crust from an honest carpenter, Bhai Lalo, milk flowed. *Langar* practice intensifies existential unity.

SEVĀ

In 2017, following Hurricane Maria, Sikhs helped restore clean drinking water to 60,000 people in Puerto Rico. This exemplifies the Sikh principle of *sevā* (community-oriented selfless service). The salient features of *sevā* are captured in a recent ethnographic study:

> Seva, as witnessed in the Sikh community . . . helps Sikhs to realize the ideals of equality and brotherhood laid down for them by the Gurus. . . . Taking part in seva done in the gurudwaras is a form of organizational religiousness.[12]

Performing actions without any selfish interest inculcates humility, develops character, and refines the five senses into the five virtues of truth, contentment, compassion, morality, and tenacity. *Sevā* inspires courageous acts to defend civil and human rights for people across castes, religions, and genders and to guard planet earth.[13]

In fact *sevā* is foreshadowed in the Japji hymn's realm of action, "where live mighty warriors and heroes" and "devotees from diverse worlds" (GGS: 8). These men and women are the courageous ethical exemplars who overcome egocentric propensities and are no longer beguiled by lust, anger, greed, attachment, or arrogance. Their hearts beat with the true One (*sacā manu soe*). Rather than an individual achievement, theirs is a collective experience. Free from all divisive and oppressive "isms" of racism, sexism, classism, religious fanaticism, these archetypal Sikh volunteers (*sevādārs*) showcased in the Japji perform joyous actions (*karahi anand*).

As noted earlier, Sikh philosophy is this-world affirming and earth oriented. "Living in this world let us serve [*vic duniā sev kamāīai*]," exhorted Guru Nanak (GGS: 26). Not confined to gurdwara precincts, ritual acts, or charity as generally conceived, *sevā* is fully integrated in engagement with the world (*vic duniā*). We hear Nanak's successors: "To serve [*sevā*] is to shed the egoistic I-me, we sing luscious praise" (GGS: 407); "when I serve [*sev*], my mind is suffused with love" (GGS: 490).

The caste-based occupations of Hindu tradition and the expected behavior for the four stages of life (*varnāshramadharma*), and for women (*stridharma*) as opposed to men, are all overthrown. The ethics of *sevā* propels Sikhs' global humanitarianism, philanthropy, and activism. *Sevā* in the form of food and shelter is extended to refugees. Gurdwaras provide services for the elderly and the needy. Sikhs run orphanages, hospitals, dispensaries, eye centers, medical colleges, and charitable trusts in many places. *Sevā* is the basis for Sikh organizations' strong leadership, social activism, humanitarian relief, and innovative advocacy. Chapters 5 and 7 provide more examples.

A contemporary example of unremitting *sevā* is the politician and social worker Jatinder Singh Shunty. At the peak of COVID-19, he took up the job of the stigmatized castes to perform the last rites of COVID-contagious patients. Unconditionally he received the dead bodies of Hindus, Muslims, Sikhs, and Christians and cremated or buried them with dignity they deserved. Actualized in his *sevā* are Guru Nanak's ideal of the One reality, *ikkoankār*, and one morality, *eko dharam*.

ANNUAL CELEBRATIONS

Ideally every moment is sacred for the Sikhs, with daily routine suffused by the religious. As we noted, Sikh scripture does not view any hour as being more auspicious than another. As a result (at least if Sikh teaching is observed), there is no reliance on horoscopes for matrimony or the start of important ventures. Guru Nanak rejected astrological charts: "We remain busy counting and determining auspicious days, but we do not know that the One Reality is above and beyond such considerations" (GGS: 904).

Nevertheless, certain days of the month and of the year have an added element of festivity or of solemnity, so Sikhs' calendar is full of celebrations. However, there is a categorical distinction between *gurpurab*s, commemorating major events in Sikh history, and *melā*s or regional cultural festivals. Since the Punjab has been predominantly an agrarian society, Sikh commemorations and celebrations are determined by the agricultural cycle and seasonal moods. As Sikhs inherited the ancient soli-lunar calendar, both the *sangrānd* (the first day of the zodiac sign) and *masiā* (the darkest night of the lunar month) are special for them.

GURPURABS

*Gurpurab*s (literally the *purab* or day of the Guru) commemorate the birthdays and death anniversaries of the ten Gurus, plus important historical events. Sikhs joyously celebrate the birth of Guru Nanak and the installation of the Guru Granth Sahib in the Harmandar. Concluding with *bhog* ceremonies on the festival morning, there are uninterrupted 48-hour readings of the Guru Granth. *Gurpurab* celebrations often include *nagar kīrtan*s (processions with colorful floats carrying the Guru Granth Sahib), and scriptural hymns are recited.

Langar is served in huge quantities. In India, wherever the procession goes, people come outside, cover their heads, remove their shoes, and pay homage to the Guru Granth Sahib. Sikh scholars are invited to gurdwaras to deliver lectures. Treasures are exhibited at the Golden Temple and other historical shrines. Prayers are said and *kaṛāh prashād* distributed. At home as well, people may have *kīrtan* and readings of the Guru Granth. Outside India, too, Sikhs celebrate, immersing themselves in their religious past, and gurdwaras invite musicians and lecturers from India and have lavish *langar*s. Often they combine religious ceremonies with intellectual and cultural events. Seminars are organized around Sikh themes in which both Sikhs and others can participate, as well as play readings, poetry, and folk dancing.

On Guru Arjan's martyrdom anniversary, which falls at the hottest time of year, *chhabīl*, a welcome drink of cold milk and water, is served. Guru Arjan is remembered for being tortured to death by being dipped in hot oil and sand. The deaths of Guru Gobind Singh's two younger sons are commemorated as martyrdoms by the thousands of devotees who gather in Fatehgarh Sahib near Sirhind in the Punjab. It was here that Zorowar Singh and Fateh Singh heroically chose to be buried alive in a brick wall rather than give up their Sikh faith. Farmers bring wheat, grain, milk, and vegetables, and everyone shares in cooking, serving, and cleaning. Devotees even stop cars and buses to offer tea and other treats to the travelers.

MELĀS

Regarding *melās*, **Baisakhi**, a spring harvest festival, often regarded as the first day of the Sikh calendar, commemorates Guru Gobind Singh's creation of the Khalsa in 1699. New members are initiated into the Khalsa community. At gurdwaras, Sikh flags are ceremonially hoisted to replace the old ones and the flagpoles are reclothed. It is regarded as an auspicious day for new undertakings and is a social, political, and religious occasion, centered especially on the city of Amritsar. From far and near, Sikhs visit the Golden Temple, and the voices of specially trained singers and musicians fill the air. The entire complex is packed with devotees bathing in the waters, listening to exegetes and musicians, preparing and partaking of *langar*, making special offerings, reverentially walking around the *parikramā* (the white marble walkway bordering the pool in which the Harmandar itself stands).

Outside the Golden Temple complex, too, farmers make the most of this time just before commencing harvesting. Goats, buffaloes, camels, and other animals are bought and sold in an annual fair. Academic functions also take place, scholars receive awards, and new books are released. As reported in chapter 2, the saddest Baisakhi festival was in 1919, and in its memory, political rallies take place at Jallianwala Bagh.

*Gurpurab*s and *melā*s offer Sikhs relaxation from work and enliven and strengthen the community as sacred space and sacred time converge.

RITES OF PASSAGE

The term "rites of passage" was coined by Dutch German French ethnographer and folklorist Arnold van Gennep in 1907 for rituals marking the individual's journey through the different stages in the life cycle. People across centuries and cultures participate in life cycle rites in different ways. According to the anthropologist Barbara Meyerhoff, these rites share an inherent universal pattern, which joins nature and culture, continuity and change, private psyche and social values.[14] In Sikhism there are four rites of passage: name giving, *amrit* initiation, marriage, and death rites.

NAME GIVING

The name-giving ritual can be extremely simple or more elaborate but basically involves naming a child in consultation with the Guru Granth Sahib. While the spine of the Guru Granth Sahib rests on the cushions, a reader (a family member if the rite is conducted in the home or an official reader if it is at the gurdwara) holds the Guru Granth Sahib closed with both hands and then gently lets it open at random. The child receives a name beginning with the first letter of the verse that appears when the Guru Granth Sahib is reverently opened. It could start on the top left of the spread or at the end of the previous page. Although nowadays some families have adopted gender-specific forenames from other cultures, traditionally Sikh forenames are unisex. The addition of the name Kaur (for girls) or Singh (for boys) indicates the gender of the child. The child also receives his or her first *kaṛā* or steel bracelet. The singing of *kīrtan* (hymns of praise), readings from the Guru Granth Sahib, recitation of *ardās* (the daily prayer), and the partaking of *langar* are the central activities, just as they are for all Sikh rites of passage.

AMRIT INITIATION

Formal initiation into the Khalsa may take place at any gurdwara and replays the event of Baisakhi 1699 recounted in chapter 1. The Guru Granth Sahib and a reader must be present and any five Sikhs (in practice males) who are already members of the Khalsa can prepare and administer the ceremony. The initiates drink *amrit* (sweetened, ritually empowered water) from their cupped hands and some is sprinkled on their eyes and hair. They also sip *amrit* from the same bowl, and together recite Guru Nanak's *mūl mantar*, remembering the One Singular Reality. The initiation marks their new birth in the Khalsa family as children of Guru Gobind Singh and his wife, Mata Sahib Kaur. The initiated are to maintain the philosophical principles enshrined in the Guru Granth Sahib and their physical identity by wearing the Five Ks: *kesh* (long, uncut hair), *kanghā* (comb to keep the hair tidy), *kirpān* (sword), *kaṛā* (bracelet), and *kacchā* (underwear). Each of them is a symbolic reminder of multivalent spiritual associations. For instance, the *kaṛā* (bracelet) is the sign par excellence of the annihilation of all occupations that determined one's place in society. Its other ascribed meanings include being a connecting link to the Divine and its circular shape is a reminder of infinity. Interestingly, nearly 200 years before Baisakhi 1699, Guru Nanak had referred to the Divine as the creator of the bracelet: "*Kari kar kartā kangan pahirai*" – "She wears the bracelet created by the Creator, so consciousness is held steadily" (GGS: 359).[15]

No particular age is prescribed for this initiation. It is open to all and may be as soon as someone can read the scripture and comprehend the articles of the Sikh faith or it may be later in life – some people wait until their own children are grown up. According to the Sikh Ethical Code (the Rahit Maryādā), "Any man or woman of whatever nationality, race, or social standing, who is prepared to accept the rules governing the Sikh community, has the right to receive amrit initiation."

ANAND KĀRAJ

The Sikh marriage rite is *anand* (bliss) *kāraj* (event). No words or gestures are directly exchanged between the bride and groom, and any legal formalities are civic, as required by their country of residence. Subsidiary rituals that are common to other Punjabis, too, include the daubing of the bride and groom with a paste (made of turmeric, flour, and mustard oil) on the day before the marriage rite, and the bride's maternal uncle giving her clothes, jewelry, and cash and adorning her with traditional red and ivory-white bangles. However, the *anand kāraj* is the sole religious Sikh solemnization. It generally takes place either in a gurdwara or in the bride's home with everyone seated on the floor facing the holy volume. The bride's father hands one end of a scarf (about two and a quarter yards long) to the groom and the other end to his daughter. Instead of exchanging wedding bands, the Sikh couple is bonded together through this auspiciously colored (pink, saffron, or red) scarf. Each holding one end of the scarf, the groom and the bride then walk around the sacred book four times. The couple's four circumambulations correspond to the four *lāvān* (circles) passages read by the *granthī* (reader of the Guru Granth Sahib).[16] As each scriptural verse is recited and then sung, the couple reverentially circumambulates the Guru Granth Sahib in a clockwise direction, the bride following the groom. Her male relatives help her around to show their support. After each circuit, the bride and groom touch the floor with their foreheads and rejoin the congregation by sitting on the floor. Bowing together to the scriptural Guru marks their acceptance of each other. They are solely – and equally – bound to the sacred word rather than to any legal or social authority. During the fourth round, the bride and groom are showered with petals by the congregation as a symbol of rejoicing. The scriptural *lāvān* launches the couple together on their spiritual journey. The British educationist Owen Cole correctly commented that "lāvān presents a reversal of the *varnāshramdharma* process by affirming that the path to *moksha* is one of deepening love, not increasing asceticism."[17] The wedding rite concludes with Amar Das's rapturous hymn, *Anand* (bliss) – the name of the wedding ceremony itself.

DEATH RITES

When a person dies, their body is bathed and dressed in clean clothes. Women who predecease their husbands wear bridal clothes. In India the dead body is carried on a bier by close male relatives and friends of the family to the funeral grounds (which are usually on the periphery of villages and towns). Unless an electric crematorium is used, it is then placed on a platform of firewood, and the eldest son (or closest male relative) lights it. The evening hymn Kirtan Sohila is recited at that point. Next, *ardās* is offered, seeking blessings for the departed person. On returning from the cremation, the participants get washed and *kaṛāh prashād* is distributed. This joyous action might appear incongruous, but it symbolically says that grief must end and normal life return once more. In Western countries the body is transported by hearse to the crematorium, and after a brief service there, the mourners proceed to the gurdwara.

After two days, family members and/or close friends return to the cremation ground/crematorium to collect the ashes and charred bones (called *phul*, literally "flowers"). These are sprinkled with milk and subsequently immersed in the flowing waters of a river or stream. The town of Kiratpur on the banks of the Sutlej in the Punjab is an esteemed site for the final immersion. In the United Kingdom, authorized locations include the river Avon beyond Stratford-upon-Avon in Warwickshire. Thus, the body returns to its constituent elements.

At the home of the deceased, the scriptural Guru takes on a central role. During the complete reading, over a number of days, family and friends congregate. They wear white, black, and earth colors, the brighter colors being reserved for weddings and other festive occasions. By sitting silently together, they share their grief and derive solace from hearing the Guru's word and sitting in its presence. A *bhog* ceremony takes place on the tenth day with the *antam ardās* (the final *ardās* prayer) recited on behalf of the deceased. On the death anniversary, the family supplies *langar* to the community.

Life and death are regarded as natural processes. Just as each day that dawns must come to an end, so must all people depart.

CULTURAL FESTIVALS

In addition to the *gurpurab*s and Baisakhi, Sikhs participate in other *melā*s, ancient Punjabi festivals to which they may give a specifically Sikh meaning.

So, Divālī short for *dīpāvalī*, literally meaning a string of lighted lamps, has been renamed Bandi Chhoṛ Divas (Prisoner Release Day), although this name is not yet as widely used as Divālī. It annually reminds Sikhs of the day their sixth Guru was released from Gwalior Fort after being imprisoned by Mughal officers under Emperor Jahangir. (For Hindus, Divālī is a major festival welcoming Lakshmi, the goddess of wealth and prosperity, and also commemorates the return of King Rama and Queen Sita to their kingdom of Ayodhya after 14 years of exile.) Houses are whitewashed and painted and decorated with earthenware lamps and candles. Gifts are exchanged and sweets are distributed.

At the Golden Temple the celebrations last for several days. The central shrine in the midst of the pool, the entire walkway, and the adjoining building are brilliantly illuminated. While electric lights and earthenware lamps filled with oil decorate the building, candles and lamps are also set afloat in the pool. As the lights on the temple are reflected in the waters, they merge splendidly with the gliding lamps. Fireworks explode to light up the night sky. Special singers and musicians are invited to perform *kīrtan* for the occasion. Lectures are delivered and heroic ballads recited. Devotees pay their respects and offer cash, flowers, *kaṛāh prashād*, rice, butter, milk, and flour. For all special celebrations, The Golden Temple's precious possessions and jewelry are displayed. Crowds come to view the golden gates, golden canopy, bejeweled peacock, pearl tassels, golden fans, and the flywhisk made up of countless hairlike fibers from sandalwood.

Lohṛī is celebrated in January when the evenings are cold. In Punjab, the tradition is for children to go around the neighborhood collecting money and sweets. Bonfires are lit and men, women, and children throw sesame seeds and peanuts into the fire and baby boys (and, increasingly, girls) are carried around it. The family of the infant's mother sends gifts and money for their son-in-law and his family. Basant is a spring festival celebrated with great joy. As though emulating the fields of brilliant yellow mustard flowers, people joyfully wear yellow and eat yellow rice. The rooftops are full of youngsters flying kites, with competitions to see who can fly their kite the highest. Part of the fun is to sabotage your opponent's kite, so boys stick ground glass to their kite strings to make them razor sharp so as to cut down competing kites.

Guru Gobind Singh gave Hindus' traditional spring festival, Holi, a distinctive Sikh form. Traditionally the playful presence of Lord Krishna is celebrated by Hindus as they splash brightly colored powders and dye on one another; they drink, gamble, and make merry. Friends and strangers alike are sprayed, splashed, and smeared with yellows, greens, reds, and blues, and social segregation dissolves. In Anandpur, Gobind Singh started the Hola Mohalla, a three-day festival during which the Sikhs trained as soldiers. Although it corresponded with the same period as Holi, the emphasis of this new festival was on physical training rather than merrymaking. There were mock battles and military exercises and contests in horsemanship, wrestling, and archery. The peaceful arts were also encouraged with competitions in music and poetry. The festival is still vigorously celebrated at Anandpur. A large fair is held annually, plus singing, discussions, and competitions in physical skill.

In August some Sikh women as well as Hindus in Punjab, and occasionally in Punjabi communities elsewhere, celebrate Tīān, as it provides a keenly awaited break from their regular routine. They receive new clothes and jewelry and wear colorful glass bangles. Girls and women exchange gifts and enjoy local fairs. Going up on swings is a big part of the traditional celebrations.

Rakhṛi (better known by its Hindi name Raksha Bandhan) is also celebrated around mid-August (on the day of the full moon). A *rakhṛī* is a bright band, usually of thread, which a sister ties around her brother's right wrist as a reminder that he is her protector. Sweets are shared, and the brother gives her money, clothes, or jewelry. In many Sikh homes, Ardās is said before the tying of the *rakhṛī*, and *kaṛāh prashād* is distributed afterward. Increasingly, however, some religious leaders condemn it as a non-Sikh festival, and so do some Sikh women as a patriarchal custom of privileging sons.

Giddhā and *bhangṛā* are popular dance performances during Sikh celebrations. *Giddhā*, danced only by women, celebrates nature's bounty through spring, summer, monsoon, autumn, and winter by capturing such simple activities as milking cows, cooking mustard seeds, sewing, fanning in the summer, buying glass bangles, churning milk in the morning, carrying water in earthenware pitchers sturdily balanced on heads, or helping with plowing and harvesting. *Bhangṛā*, which was traditionally performed by men, dates back to the 14th century, originating in West Punjab (now in Pakistan).[18] Today *bhangṛā* is popular with both Sikh men and women. Dressed in bright colors, the group dances in an elemental rhythm to the beat of a large drum, and everybody joins in the songs celebrating Punjabi village life. With the migration of Sikh communities to the West, this Punjabi folk dance is popular in Britain, Europe, and North America. The modern form of *bhangṛā* combines North Indian folk music with contemporary styles including reggae and Western pop while also being a crucial marker of Sikh memory and identity. The lyrics are often distinctly macho, and the gendered nature of these popular Punjabi festivities will be revisited in chapter 7.

CONCLUSION

More generally, the divergence today between the Gurus' emphases and Sikhs' actual behavior illustrates their implication in the dynamic tensions between, first, *the Sikh religion* itself (the message of the Gurus and its subsequent formulation in codes of discipline) and, second, ***panjābīat*** ("Punjabiness," a cultural mix of patriarchy and often competitive concern with family honor, plus of course Punjabi language, cuisine, dress, humor, and celebration). A third factor in Sikhs' behavior is modernity in the sense of secular, more individualistic "Western" values. Arguably the tensions are most challenging for young people in their teens and 20s, particularly for women, and most especially for those living in Western countries, where these three pressures of the Sikh religion, *panjābīat*, and modernity can at times seem irreconcilable. At the same time, it needs to be acknowledged that in some situations two or more of these factors will reinforce each other. So, for example, those who wish to marry a person of lower caste may draw strength both from the religion's emphasis on a caste-free society and from the irrelevance of caste divisions in modern Western society, though at the same time they risk incurring censure or exclusion for jeopardizing family honor, a powerful element in *panjābīat*. When, however, it comes to the matter of philanthropy, such as substantial contributions to projects in overseas Sikhs' ancestral villages, not only the Sikh religion and modernity but also Punjab's cultural values combine to encourage diaspora Sikhs to give generously – as evidenced by, for example, the multitude of Sikh religious buildings all over Punjab that overseas Sikhs have funded, often in memory of deceased family members.

This chapter has provided a general framework for the Sikh religion's emphasis on being alive to the singular infinite Divine throughout each day and season, as envisioned by Guru Nanak and successive Gurus. Accordingly, Guru Granth Sahib is the nub of Sikh personal and collective existence, with life centered on the physical presence of the scriptural volume. However, Sikh behavior often deviates from the liberating ideology that it contains, and chapter 7 will consider some of the challenges that these discrepancies pose.

NOTES

1 For a detailed analysis of *akhaṇḍ pāṭh*, see Kristina Myrvold, *Inside the Guru's Gate: Ritual Uses of Texts among the Sikhs in Varanasi* (Lund: Lund University, 2007), 269.
2 Victor Turner, *The Ritual Process: Structure and Anti-Structure* (Chicago: Aldine, 1969), 132.
3 Émile Durkheim, *The Elementary Forms of Religious Life*, trans. J.W. Swain (London: Allen & Unwin, [1912] 1976), 216–217.

4 B.N. Goswamy and Caron Smith, *I See No Stranger: Early Sikh Art and Devotion* (New York: Rubin Museum of Art, 2006); Valarie Kaur, *See No Stranger* (New York: One World, 2020).
5 Piar Singh, ed., *B-40 Janamsakhi Sri Guru Nanak Devji* (Amritsar: Guru Nanak Dev University, 2009), 133. For detailed discussion, see Nikky-Guninder Kaur Singh, *Janamsakhi: Paintings of Guru Nanak in Early Sikh Art* (New Delhi: Roli, 2023), 165–167.
6 Piar Singh, *B-40 Janamsakhi Sri Guru Nanak Devji*, 91.
7 Lydia Polgreen, "A Sikh Temple Where All May Eat, and Pitch In," *New York Times*, August 29, 2010.
8 Controversially, some gurdwaras have introduced tables and chairs in their *langar* halls.
9 Colorado Sikhs and University of Denver Staff, "How Did Langar Become the Basis for a University Course?" *SikhNet*, March 14, 2002, https://www.sikhnet.com/news/how-did-Langar-become-basis-university-course.
10 Nikky-Guninder Kaur Singh, "Translating Sikh Scripture: Rebounding Sound and Sense," *The Routledge Handbook of Translation and Religion*, ed. Hephzibah Israel (Abingdon: Routledge, 2023), 480–494.
11 Isabel Wilkerson, *Caste: The Origins of our Discontents* (New York: Random House, 2020).
12 Khushbeen Kaur Sohi, Purnima Singh, and Krutika Bopanna, "Ritual Participation, Sense of Community, and Social Well-Being: A Study of Seva in the Sikh Community," *Journal of Religion and Health* 57, no. 6 (2018): 2066–2078, 2074.
13 Nikky-Guninder Kaur Singh, *First Sikh: Life and Legacy of Guru Nanak* (New Delhi: Penguin Random House, 2019), 189–207.
14 Barbara Meyeroff in Victor Turner, *Celebration: Studies in Festivity and Ritual* (Washington, DC: Smithsonian Institution Press, 1982), 109–135.
15 For more details, see Nikky-Guninder Kaur Singh, *The Birth of the Khalsa: A Feminist Re-memory of Sikh Identity* (Albany: State University of New York Press, 2005), chap. 4.
16 For more on Sikh weddings, see chapter 7.
17 Owen Cole, *The Sikhs: Their Religious Beliefs and Practices* (Brighton: Sussex Academy Press, 1995), 124.
18 See Anjali Gera Roy, *Bhangra Moves: From Ludhiana to London and Beyond* (Aldershot: Ashgate, 2010).

REFERENCES AND FURTHER READING

Mooney, Nicola. "'In Our Whole Society, There Is No Equality': Sikh Householding and the Intersection of Gender and Caste." *Religions* 11, no. 2 (2020): 95.

Myrvold, Kristina. *Inside the Guru's Gate: Ritual Uses of Texts among the Sikhs in Varanasi*. Lund: Lund University, 2007.

Singh, Nikky-Guninder Kaur. "Sikh Scriptemics during Pandemic." In *The Covid Pandemic and the World's Religions Challenges and Responses*, 105–112. London: Bloomsbury Press, 2023.

Singh, Nikky-Guninder Kaur. "Why Did I Not Light Up the Pyre? The Refeminization of Ritual in Sikhism." *Journal of Feminist Studies in Religion* 16, no. 1 (2000): 63–85.

Takhar, Opinderjit, and Doris Jakobsh (eds.). *Global Sikhs: Histories, Practices and Identities*. Abingdon: Routledge, 2023.

5

SIKH DIASPORA

INTRODUCTION

Vishvajit Singh is the subject of *American Sikh*, an award-winning animated film released in 2023. Born in the United States, he grew up in New Delhi where, in November 1984, he experienced the horrific massacre of Sikhs that followed the killing of Prime Minister Indira Gandhi. When, in the 1990s, he returned to the United States, he was taunted as a "raghead" and told to "go back home," with the result that he removed his turban, had his hair cut, and shaved off his beard. This worsened his identity crisis, and so in 2001 he again became a turban-wearing Sikh, only to find, in November that same year, that this marked him out as not only an outsider but also as an enemy in the aftermath of the Islamists' assault on the Twin Towers. In 2014, the documentary *Red, White, and Beard* showcased Vishvajit Singh as a cartoonist who had created "Sikh Captain America" as a new take on the original Captain America. For this new incarnation the enemy was not the Nazis but intolerance in US society.

There are no reliable numbers for Sikhs who, like Vishvajit Singh, are living outside India, as the category of "Sikh" does not appear on most national censuses. However, more than one in ten Sikhs are estimated to be living in other countries and "Sikh **diaspora**" is the term that is generally used to refer to them.[1] This chapter offers an overview of Sikh migration and settlement – its geographic spread and its principal phases and characteristics. Specific detail, like Vishvajit Singh's story, will convey a little of the unique and diverse character of some

DOI: 10.4324/9781003359210-5

countries' Sikh communities, the existential challenges that individuals have faced, and the ways in which Sikh communities have developed over time in far-flung locations and enriched the societies in which they live.

Before proceeding, however, we need to consider more critically the meaning of the term "diaspora." This process will help us to approach the Sikh case more analytically. A substantial body of scholarly literature focuses not only on particular diasporas (e.g., the Jewish diaspora or the Armenian diaspora) but also on the usage of the term itself. Interested readers are recommended to look at discussions by the sociologist Martin Baumann,[2] the anthropologist Steven Vertovec,[3] and the Sikh studies specialist Darshan Singh Tatla,[4] among others. Baumann usefully identified three related meanings of the word "diaspora": the process of becoming scattered, the actual community that finds itself living overseas, and the geographic space in which dispersed groups reside. Other scholars have identified the push factors (such as poverty) and pull factors (like plentiful employment in the destination country) that constitute the dispersion process.

Tatla argues that (as with the dispersal of the Jewish people, the first dispersal of people of a particular faith to be called a diaspora) a key element of diaspora is trauma in one's homeland – in the Sikh case, he argued (even though Sikhs had been emigrating for over 50 years before this date), these were the events of 1984. The Sikhs' trauma was the storming of Harmandar Sahib and the killing of Sikhs in North India following the assassination of Prime Minister Indira Gandhi – and the community's indelibly scarring memory of these events. Tatla cites too the characteristics that the social scientist Robin Cohen suggested in order for migrant communities to "gain diaspora status." As well as "dispersal from an original homeland, often traumatically" or, alternatively, "expansion from a homeland, in search of work, in pursuit of trade or to further colonial ambitions," these characteristics include "a collective memory and myth about the homeland" and "the development of a return movement."

Whether we use the term "diaspora" or speak of overseas Sikhs in other ways – for example, as migrants and minorities in various countries – it may be more appropriate to think increasingly in terms of a single transnational, global Sikh community, interconnected across borders in multiple ways – and more strongly connected than ever before thanks to communications media. In fact, one area of contemporary research is the digital Sikh diaspora.

For over 200 years, some Sikhs have been living outside India. Reasons for leaving India and for settling in a particular country vary, but in most cases, there has been a strong economic motivation. Emigrés' remittances to Punjab have contributed significantly to their families' financial standing as well as paying for more family members to emigrate. Meanwhile, overseas Sikhs have been active in maintaining their religion despite the often challenging conditions that they faced in the "host" country. They have, at the same time, participated in political movements relating to their homeland. The history of Sikh settlement in each overseas locale is different, but there has been a tendency for migration to proceed in phases, with the first arrivals being men of working age, who worked in low-paid occupations and were subsequently joined by their wives. Through hard work and a commitment to education, the first generation then enabled their children to gain professional employment. This upward mobility has seen Sikhs integrating in local society, though often against a backdrop of racial discrimination, and as Vertovec has pointed out, increasing integration does not necessarily mean a decrease in attachment to homeland.

The gurdwaras that Sikhs have established worldwide confidently map their presence and facilitate religious and cultural continuity. We will see how the Guru Granth Sahib has traveled to far destinations; gurdwaras have grown from small rooms to multimillion-pound architectural landmarks; internationally peripatetic *sant*s (spiritual leaders) and ***rāgī***s (devotional musicians) have quickened and deepened Sikhs' religious commitment; and disputes centered on the right to wear turbans and bear *kirpān*s have recurrently drawn the attention of the news media. Matters of Sikh ***rahit*** (discipline) (such as the provision – or not – of seating in the gurdwara, or the requirements of *anand kāraj* marriage) have been hotly contested in the diaspora. At the same time, local and global disasters have given rise to a surge of public service so that Sikhs' commitment to *sevā* has a higher profile than ever before.

This chapter briefly traces some country-specific histories of Sikh migration to countries in Asia, Australasia, Africa, America, and Europe. One notes the interplay of caste, class, and other factors, as well as the role of national legislation regarding race and immigration. The very different local opportunities for employment have included fruit farming in California, cheese making in Italy, and moneylending in the Philippines.

Sikh tradition enshrines stories of Guru Nanak's travels beyond Punjab – reputedly as far as Mecca, Sri Lanka, Assam, and Tibet – in order to spread his message. Until the 19th century, however, Sikhs had little incentive or opportunity to travel beyond the Indian subcontinent. This was to change with the British East India Company's annexation of Punjab in 1849 and the absorption of Punjab into the British Empire, which in turn resulted in thousands of Sikh men traveling overseas. Even before this, some Sikh men had already been recruited by the British to serve in the police in China.

From 1849, Sikh political prisoners were dispatched to Singapore, which was at that time serving the British as a penal colony. Generally, however, men have left Punjab for better livelihoods. This was the case, too, with the internal migration of Sikh agriculturalists in the 19th century from relatively congested areas of East Punjab, when the British improved the irrigation in West Punjab (now in Pakistan) and set up canal colonies there. By the 1890s, as **indentured laborers**, Sikh men were laying the railway that would link Kenya and Uganda. Others were serving in the British Indian Army for which Sikhs were favored recruits. Military service took Sikh soldiers to, among other places, China, North Africa, and Western Europe, and it opened their eyes to longer term possibilities outside India. More permanent migrations, which continued after Indian independence, were most often motivated by the hope of working to improve their families' prospects, though in some cases in the second half of the 20th century, as we shall see, Sikhs were fleeing discrimination or violence, whether in East Africa, North India, or Afghanistan.

The demography of Sikh settlement outside India is changing and is likely to continue to do so. Thus, whereas the once-flourishing Sikh population of Afghanistan has all but disappeared, numbers of Sikh residents in, among other countries, Canada, Italy, and Australia are increasing.

ASIA, AUSTRALASIA, AND AFRICA

Sikhs have migrated from India to several other parts of Asia. Moreover, the first Sikhs in Afghanistan are claimed to have been local people who were won over by the preaching of Guru Nanak himself. Their descendants were augmented in the 19th century by Sikh merchants during the later Sikh empire. Sadly, the international news channel Al Jazeera reported, in January 2022, following the withdrawal of US forces and the resurgence of the Taliban, that the population of possibly several hundred thousand in the 1970s had dwindled to an estimated 140 individuals as a result of persecution under Taliban rule and Sikhs' resultant emigration, mostly to India.[5]

Farther east, the history of Sikhs in China (beginning similarly, according to tradition, with Guru Nanak's visit to Tibet) includes an encounter during the Sino-Sikh War of 1841–1842 and Sikh soldiers' service during the Second Opium War (1856–1860) as well as during the Boxer Rebellion in 1900.[6] In 1867, 100 Sikh police arrived in Hong Kong, and Sikhs were similarly recruited to police Shanghai (where there was a British settlement from 1845 to 1863) and to maintain law and order in other British dominions such as British Malaya and Burma (now Malaysia and Myanmar). After several phases of migration, Malaysia's population now includes around 65,000 Sikhs, working in a wide range of occupations, and there are well over 100 gurdwaras. Medan, the capital of neighboring North Sumatra in Indonesia, has a long-established Sikh population whose first members came not as police but as dairy farmers and businessmen. In Myanmar, however, because of ongoing discrimination (e.g., Sikh candidates are not allowed to wear a turban for their examinations), Sikh numbers have dwindled to perhaps 2,000–3,000 Sikhs. By contrast, Thailand's Sikhs have primarily been successful entrepreneurs and are an influential business community. Many migrated to Thailand from West Punjab (now in Pakistan) because of the partition of India in 1947 and joined a Thai Sikh community that had already been trading in Thailand for about 150 years. Sikhism is now recognized as one of Thailand's five major religions.

Regarding West Asia, *janamsākhī* accounts tell of Guru Nanak's visit to Mecca, and his visit to Baghdad (dated to 1511–1513) was marked by a gurdwara that was identified by a Sikh who was serving with the British army in Iraq during the First World War. Subsequently, during the Second World War, Sikh soldiers restored the building. From the 1960s, Sikh contractual laborers worked on construction sites in Iraq, the United Arab Emirates, Oman, Saudi Arabia, and Bahrain. Sikh communities continue to live in all these countries apart from Iraq, where the region's one historical gurdwara was all but destroyed during warfare in 2003.

The first Sikhs probably reached Australia in the 1830s. Subsequently, camel drivers came to Australia in the 1860s: although most camel drivers were Muslims, some were Sikhs. Later, Australians became familiar with the arrival on their doorsteps of Sikh hawkers who supplied far-flung households with a wide range of items. Whereas many Sikhs subsequently came from India, others migrated from Malaya and Hong Kong. Then, with hostility against Asian immigrants increasing, the 1901 Immigration Restriction Act was passed to prevent further migration from Asia. As a result, Sikh immigration was curbed until the 1970s when new immigration legislation focused more on potential migrants' skills than on their ethnicity. With a population of 210,000 reported in the 2021 census, Sikhs are now the fastest growing faith community in Australia, especially due to the migration of thousands of students.

An early record of Sikhs in New Zealand dates from 1888 when the *Otago Daily Times* mentioned a Sikh candy seller, but this was 70 years after Indians had first landed in New Zealand. However, New Zealand was slower than Australia to implement anti-Asian legislation, although from 1899 successive laws discriminated against Asian migration until, as recently as 1987, an immigration review advocated removing ethnicity and nationality as considerations in assessing potential migrants.

In the 1890s the British were not only ruling India but also creating a British protectorate out of their sphere of influence in East Africa, and they needed skilled construction workers to lay the railway from Mombasa to Lake Victoria. Knowing the expertise of Indian carpenters, blacksmiths, masons, and bricklayers, they drafted in indentured laborers from India's two western states of Gujarat and Punjab. Sikhs from these construction-related hereditary communities had adopted the caste name of Ramgarhia (the title of their distinguished 18th-century Sikh leader Jassa Singh Ramgarhia). When their three-year term of indenture ended, a minority stayed on, realizing the business opportunities, and they were joined by more Sikhs who moved from Punjab to East Africa. East Africa's Sikhs prospered in a range of occupations as a middle tier in colonial society, between the indigenous Africans and their British rulers. One Indian-born Kenyan Sikh, Makhan Singh, is remembered as a labor union leader who reputedly laid the foundations of trade unionism in Kenya. As a punishment, he suffered 11 years' detention by the British authorities.

Prospects for the Sikhs, and other "Asians," worsened when in 1961, 1962, and 1963, respectively, Tanzania, Uganda, and Kenya became independent. Notoriously, in August 1972, following a dream, Uganda's president Idi Amin expelled all Asians. Many had already emigrated from all three countries as non-African nationals had been disadvantaged by the countries' Africanization policies. As they were already "Citizens of the UK and Colonies," most East African Asians came to the United Kingdom, while a smaller number shifted to India and some of the better-qualified moved to Canada and the United States.

NORTH AMERICA

Sikhs had begun settling in North America much earlier in the 20th century than the arrivals from East Africa. Indeed, the first four Sikhs had reached California in 1899. In California Sikh settlers (in the first instance soldiers from the Far East) worked as farmers and fruit growers, and currently 50 percent of the US Sikh population live in California, with most in Yuba City.

As early as 1887 a Sikh regiment, traveling to India from Queen Victoria's Golden Jubilee in London, had visited Canada and seen a land of opportunity. Canada's lumber industry was to offer jobs to many Sikhs, and between 1903 and 1908, British

Columbia's Sikh population grew from 300 to 5,000. Over a century later most Canadian Sikhs still live in British Columbia.

In both Canada and the United States, Sikhs ("Hindoos," as they were known for many years) faced discrimination. In the United States, they were not allowed to bring in wives from Punjab and they were also forbidden to marry white women. As a result, Sikhs married Mexican women and their children grew up as Spanish-speaking Roman Catholics.[7] Racist legislation restricted Sikh immigration to both Canada and the United States, and immigrants faced discrimination.

In fact, it took the Sikh writer and First World War veteran Bhagat Singh Thind nearly 20 years to be granted naturalization in 1935 as a US citizen, as he did not qualify as either a "white person" or a "person of African descent." Thind supported the principle of Indian independence, but he had not participated in the Ghadar (rebellion) movement of Indian (mainly Sikh) revolutionaries based in North America.

The Ghadarites' agitation had climaxed in the *Komagata Maru* incident, a major confrontation in Vancouver in 1914 on the arrival of a Japanese ship, the *Komagata Maru.* [8] It had been chartered by Gurdit Singh, a Singapore-based entrepreneur, to bring mainly Sikh would-be immigrants to Canada. The 376 passengers (including 340 Sikhs) arrived at Victoria Harbor, but with the exception of just a handful, they were barred from entry by the prejudicial policies of the Canadian immigration office. After its passengers were refused entry, the ship sailed back to Calcutta where – as alleged revolutionaries – some returnees were shot and others were imprisoned.

It was only in the 1960s that both Canada and the United States opened up immigration from India, so allowing a major influx, including many professionals. Sikhs, such as the one-time Canadian MP Ujjal Singh (2004–2011), and people of Sikh background, such as Nikki Haley, who became the first female governor of South Carolina (2011–2017) and subsequently the US ambassador to the United Nations (2017–2018), continue to make their mark at the highest levels. In July 2024, two days after an assassination attempt on the Republican presidential nominee Donald Trump, Harmeet Dhillon, a Sikh Republican leader, faced social media trolling after reciting a Sikh prayer at the Republican National Convention. The prayer, the Ardās, provoked controversy among some far-right Christian circles who criticized its inclusion at a predominantly Christian event. By 2019 Canada had 18 Sikh MPs. (At that time, India's Lok Sabha had only 13 Sikh members.) Distinguished North American Sikhs include "the father of fiberoptics," the American physicist, entrepreneur, and philanthropist Narinder Singh Kapany (1926–2020) and the Canadian author Shauna Singh Baldwin.

Sadly, as Vishvajit Singh's experience illustrated, the story of Sikhs in North America has not been one of straightforward integration, upward mobility, and success. In Canada there has been ongoing controversy relating to many Canadian Sikhs' support for the Khalistan movement and a few Sikhs' consequent implication in the downing of Air India Flight 182 in 1985. In the United States the 9/11 assault on the Twin Towers in New York in 2001 increased Islamophobic hate crime, and in many cases turbaned and bearded Sikh men were mistaken for Muslims and assaulted. The first post-9/11 victim was Balbir Singh Sodhi, a Sikh petrol station owner, who was murdered soon after. Then, in 2012, a white supremacist opened fire in the Oak Creek gurdwara in Wisconsin, killing six worshippers and wounding four others. What's more, Sikhs, like other minorities, suffered from the racial tension that was ramped up during the presidency of Donald Trump, 2017–2021.

One positive outcome of this negativity has been the emergence of strong Sikh American civil rights organizations, including SALDEF (Sikh American Legal Defense and Education Fund), SMART (Sikh Mediation and Rehabilitation Team), United Sikhs (a United Nations–associated international advocacy organization that operates in ten countries), and Sikh Coalition. American Sikh activists reach out to educate the wider public about Sikhs and Sikh values, emphasizing how they uphold key American values such as liberty and service.

EUROPE

THE UNITED KINGDOM

Probably twice as many Sikhs live in the United Kingdom as in the whole of the rest of Europe, and the start of Sikh migration to the United Kingdom preceded by several decades any sustained attempt to settle in mainland European countries, so it is with Sikhs in the United Kingdom that this section begins.[9] Together with Canada and the United States, the United Kingdom is home to one of the three biggest Sikh populations outside India.

The story of Sikh migration to the United Kingdom began with royalty. In 1854 the deposed maharaja of Punjab, Duleep Singh, was exiled to Britain and spent most of his life there as Queen Victoria's increasingly disillusioned protégé: her journal not only describes her meetings with him but also includes little watercolor sketches of him. Years later, Victoria employed Bhai Ram Singh (the first Ramgarhia Sikh to come to Britain) from Lahore to design an oriental room in her palace on the Isle of Wight (see chapter 6). The maharaja of Patiala was another visitor, and he endowed the Central London Gurdwara, which opened in 1911. Wealthy families began sending their sons from Punjab to study in British universities.

Between the World Wars, Sikh men of the Bhatra caste settled mostly in British seaports such as Southampton and Glasgow. The first Bhatra settlers were men who worked as peddlers of clothing and haberdashery, and until the 1980s, Bhatra women were discouraged from higher education and from working outside the home. Nowadays both men and women aspire to professional employment, and the previously stigmatized community increasingly identifies as "Bhat," so marking a connection with the bardic contributors to the Guru Granth Sahib.

In addition to ties that stemmed from the imperial relationship between Britain and the Sikhs, larger scale migration was driven by economics, notably by the dwindling land inheritances for peasant farmers in Punjab's Jalandhar Doab area and by the social pressure to boost family finances, including meeting the cost of daughters' marriages. This push factor, and the sense of upheaval that followed the partition of India in 1947, coincided with the pull of a demand for labor in postwar Britain. Subsequent political factors in Sikhs' migration to the United Kingdom include (as we have already noted) the Africanization policies from the 1960s in East African countries plus the unrest in Punjab that climaxed in 1984 in the Indian army's action in Harmandar Sahib and in the killing of Prime Minister Indira

Gandhi in New Delhi and the pogrom that ensued, as well as the intensification of the civil war in Afghanistan and discrimination against non-Muslims after the collapse of Mohammed Najibullah's government in 1992.

From the early 1950s, Sikhs of the Jat (peasant landowner) caste, mainly from the districts of Jalandhar and Hoshiarpur, settled in considerable numbers in Greater London as well as in industrial cities in northern England and the Midlands where there were plenty of vacancies in foundries and factories. During the same period, members of a more stigmatized, non-landowning caste, the Ravidasis (or Ravidassias), also arrived. Around 1970, as noted above, Ramgarhia Sikhs arrived from Uganda, Kenya, and Tanzania, adding to the numbers of Ramgarhias who had already migrated directly from India. Then, in the 1990s, Afghan Sikhs came and settled in Southall (in Greater London). There is also an unknown number of undocumented Sikh migrants, overstayers, and asylum seekers and their numbers would have been swelled by extensive internal migration when the United Kingdom was still a member of the European Union.

In hopes of restricting the numbers of Sikhs and other Commonwealth citizens entering the United Kingdom, successive immigration acts were passed, starting with the Commonwealth Immigrants Acts of 1962 and 1968 and the Immigration Act 1971. Nonetheless, Sikhs have continued to migrate to the United Kingdom, and the Sikh population figures in England and Wales in the 2021 census were 524,000. There are probably over 300 gurdwaras.

Sikhs are making their mark in British society as MPs (12, half of them women, were elected in 2024, and Tanmanjeet Singh Dhesi, the first turbaned Sikh MP, was elected as chair of the Defence Committee) and also as members of the House of Lords. Every year there are Sikhs whose achievements are honored by the award of MBEs (Members of the Order of the British Empire) and OBEs (Officers of the Order of the British Empire). Sikhs are represented in interfaith groups and as members of hospital and prison chaplaincy teams. For many years Sikhism has had a place in the syllabi of the statutory curriculum subject of religious education.

MAINLAND EUROPE

Turning from Britain to mainland Europe, it is true that two Sikh princes, Duleep Singh (Maharaja Ranjit Singh's son) and Jagatjit Singh (maharaja of Kapurthala), spent time there during the 19th century and also that thousands of Sikhs served – and died – in the British army in Western Europe in both World Wars.[10] In Germany in the First World War, Umrao Singh Majithia, a young Sikh intellectual, supported not the British but the India-Germany group which was conspiring against the British, intending to invade India via Afghanistan.

However, despite Sikhs' early 20th-century wartime experiences in Western Europe, Sikh settlement in mainland European countries only really got underway in the 1970s. Many Sikhs were economic migrants from Punjab, while others (in parallel with the phases of Sikhs' migration to the United Kingdom) came as refugees and asylum seekers, first from Uganda, then from Punjab itself, and most recently, from Afghanistan. The ending of the Cold War, with the fall of the Soviet Union, facilitated migration as new routes opened up. Additionally, there were routes via North Africa's Spanish territories, and via Turkey into Greece, and Afghan Sikhs got to Russia by way of Tajikistan, Kyrgyzstan, and Kazakhstan. The number of Sikh students at European universities continues to increase as well, with Poland, for example, being popular as a relatively inexpensive destination. New primary migration includes Sikh professionals coming to Northern and Western Europe to work in information technology, telecommunications, and health care.

Population figures are unreliable, not only because many national censuses do not ask for people's religion but also because many Sikhs are undocumented migrants. According to one informed estimate in 2020, the total number of Sikhs in mainland Europe was possibly fewer than 250,000, with the largest concentrations in Italy (which had over 40 gurdwaras), plus Germany and Greece, followed by the Netherlands, France, and Spain. Within individual countries, too, Sikh populations tend to be locally concentrated, with many of Spain's Sikhs living in Barcelona and most of France's in Paris and its northern and eastern suburbs. Sikhs are also concentrated in certain occupations: Italy initially became an attractive option as Italian regulations allowed the immigration of those who claimed to be circus personnel and Italy's Sikhs have since become synonymous with dairy work and cheese production. Internal migration occurs within Europe, especially as Sikhs in poorer countries such as Portugal try to move to the more affluent countries of Northern and Western Europe.

Sikhs' religious customs are adapting to new settings: for example, in Sweden, to satisfy legal requirements, a Christian priest conducts a short ceremony to legalize Sikhs' marriage, and cremations are carried out in rooms under the supervision of the Church of Sweden and funeral directors. At the same time, Sikhs are organizing so as to represent their interests and to educate a wider public about their religion and culture. For instance, Norwegian Sikhs organize turban days near the Baisakhi festival in April when everyone can experiment with wearing a turban and can receive information about Sikhism. Meanwhile, alongside such initiatives in building mutual understanding, the many illegal migrants' situation remains precarious, with undocumented Sikhs in Italy, for example, living under the thumb of gang masters who recruit farm laborers for landowners. Moreover, unease over the external indicators of Sikhs' religious identity surface from time to time both in European countries and elsewhere.

TURBAN AND *KIRPĀN* DISPUTES

Thus, when in 2004, a French law – primarily aimed at Muslims – banned religious symbols in state schools, Sikh students could no longer wear a turban or a *paṭkā* (a simpler head covering). More generally, turban-wearing Sikhs in European countries have experienced discrimination, especially since 9/11, and especially from various countries' border controls. For instance, in 2011 the hydrologist Dr. Shaminder Puri lost his legal challenge to the Polish airport authorities for repeatedly requiring him to remove his turban. Change occurs gradually: the organization United Sikhs successfully challenged France's ban on turbans in public schools and in photographs on IDs and also, in Belgium, the ban on wearing a *paṭkā* in schools; Italian Sikhs are now allowed to wear turbans for their ID photographs, and after a six-year campaign, Norwegian Sikhs are now permitted to have passport photos that do not show their ears (a requirement incompatible with tying a turban appropriately, except in the style adopted by Namdhari Sikhs).

Sikhs in many other countries, too, have come to public notice in a succession of disputes and legal cases centered on the right to wear the turban. In the United Kingdom, in 1976, the Motor Cycle Crash Helmets (Religious Exemption) Act was a victory for Sikhs to wear a turban rather than the mandatory crash helmet – a mainly symbolic victory as, in practice, so few Sikhs used motor cycles. Before this, attention had focused on the right of uniformed bus crews to have beards and turbans. In Wolverhampton, Sikh bus crews were successful in 1969, and in 1976 permission was granted to Manchester busmen after over a decade's struggle.

In the same year Britain's Sikhs gained protection (similar to Jews' already well-established legal protection) under the Race Relations Act 1976. This resulted from the definition of "ethnoreligious" in the *Mandla vs. Dowell Lee* case. This case involved not a bus company but an independent school which had made a Sikh boy's place conditional on his removing his turban. Subsequent campaigning for turbaned Sikh workers on construction sites to be exempted from the requirement to wear a hard hat led to their exemption in the Employment Act 1989. This was in turn amended by Section 6 of the Deregulation Act 2015 exempting turban-wearing Sikhs from any legal requirement to wear head protection at a workplace. The Equalities Act 2010 had already made it unlawful to discriminate against anyone on the grounds of race or religious belief and placed a duty on public bodies to promote racial equality.

In Canada it was not until 1990 that an officer in the iconic Royal Canadian Mounted Police won the right to wear a turban while on duty.

As it is carried only by *amritdhāri* Sikhs, and often inconspicuously, the *kirpān* (sword) has been a less frequent cause of tension. Disputes, whether in schools, prisons, or airports, have in most cases been settled amicably. Nonetheless, Sikhs' right to carry a *kirpān* has been challenged across the globe. *Cheema v.*

Thompson was a high-profile case in California, where carrying knives with blades longer that two and a half inches on school premises was illegal. Legal action began in the early 1990s when a group of pupils, who had been suspended by the Livingston Union School District for wearing a *kirpān*, sued the district under the Religious Freedom Restoration Act. Eventually in 2020, the Central Unified School District considered allowing Sikh pupils to retain their *kirpān* in school but only on strict conditions.

Moreover, to take just two European examples: in 2006 a Danish court confirmed a ban on Sikhs carrying a ceremonial knife, and in 2017 Italy's Supreme Court ruled that public safety superseded an individual's rights. However, under Swiss law a *kirpān* is not technically a weapon, as its blade is asymmetric, there is no automatic switching mechanism, and it is not a throwing knife.

In 2008 in the United Kingdom, the *kaṛā* too made legal history with the judge's ruling, in the *Watkins-Singh v. Aberdare Girls' High School* case, that a school in Wales was guilty of indirect discrimination under race relations and equality laws for requiring a girl to remove her *kaṛā* in line with its "no jewelry" policy.

GURDWARAS AND RELIGIOUS SOCIALIZATION

Whereas Sikhs overseas have faced sporadic discrimination with regard to maintaining these outward indicators of their faith, their gurdwaras, centered on their Guru, the enthroned Guru Granth Sahib, have provided venues in which Sikhs can confidently maintain their distinctive identity and way of worship as well as socialize. In the early years of settlement, a local community's gurdwara opens in existing premises that have been adapted for the purpose. As the community grows, it may establish an impressive, distinctively domed building. In either case, it is marked by a *nishān sahib*, the pennant bearing the characteristic *khaṇḍā* emblem consisting of a two-edged sword bisecting a quoit and cupped by two *kirpāns*. In 2024, to mark the distinctiveness of Sikh tradition from Hindu tradition, the Akāl Takht ruled that the pennant's color must be *basantī* (yellow) or *surmāī* (navy blue) rather than the prevalent saffron color.

Figure 5.1 Khaṇḍā emblem consisting of three swords and a quoit

The first overseas gurdwaras opened in Kenya in 1892, in Myanmar (Burma as it was at that time) in 1897, in Hong Kong in 1901, in Vancouver in 1907, and in London in 1911. Gurdwaras provide a religious focus, as the location for daily worship, for marriages and funeral-related observances, and for the celebration of festivals. They are also community centers that provide informal and formal support. They are venues for advice on health and immigration, for language tuition, and music classes that teach the skills necessary for *kīrtan* – singing *shabad*, playing the tablā and harmonium,[11] and increasingly, the more traditional stringed instruments that the harmonium displaced in British India (see chapter 7). What is more, gurdwaras are a point of contact for outsiders: in the United Kingdom, for example, gurdwaras are visited by classes from local schools and by interfaith groups wishing to learn about the Sikh religion.

The Guru Granth Sahib is central to every gurdwara, as well as being housed in private homes that can accommodate it appropriately. Each copy has been produced under the auspices of the Akāl Takht either by the Shiromani Gurdwara Parbandhak Committee Press in Ramsar Gurdwara in Amritsar or by the Delhi Gurdwara Parbandhak Committee Press in Rakabganj Gurdwara in New Delhi and has then been reverently borne to its eventual overseas destination. For example, in April 2004, 149 copies of Guru Granth Sahib arrived in Toronto from Amritsar by a chartered flight, with each copy duly occupying a separate seat. Attempts by Sikhs in British Columbia to produce copies locally have not been approved by the Akāl Takht.

One ongoing issue for diaspora Sikhs is how best to observe Sikh *maryādā* (discipline) while also accommodating worshippers who are unable to sit on the floor in the ***divān*** hall (as is required in the presence of the Guru Granth Sahib) and in the *langar*. In 1997 a *hukamnāmā* prohibited the use of chairs and tables in the *langar*, and the following year six Canadian Sikhs were excommunicated for disobeying. Increasingly, widespread compromises now allow for the more elderly and infirm to sit on a cushioned bench along the back wall of the *divān* hall and to use chairs and tables in the *langar* (surprisingly chairs and tables for *langar* are now very common in the United States for the old and young alike). In 2013 a directive from Amritsar required any gurdwara seating for elderly or disabled people to be on verandas, with the religious service relayed there via screens. Interestingly, by contrast with such regulations, a century earlier, when North America's first, still-existing gurdwara, Stockton gurdwara, was established in 1912, not only had worshippers kept their shoes on and sat on chairs in the *divān*, but (influenced by Christian church convention), the male worshippers left their headgear on hatstands on entering the building.

Sikhs' marriages outside India are increasingly not only inter-caste but also with non-Sikhs (most often families of Hindu or Christian heritage), with some Sikhs marrying partners from a non–South Asian background. In 2007 a *sandesh* (a ruling from the SGPC) clarified that *anand kāraj* could only be conducted between Sikhs. Non-Sikhs must first adopt Sikh faith and, as evidence of this, must have Kaur or Singh in their name on identity documents. The solemnization of many mixed marriages in the United Kingdom was aggressively disrupted, with the result that in 2014, guidance issued by the Sikh Council stated that marriages in gurdwaras could only be between two Sikhs. While some Sikhs are dismayed by the negative impact of this on families of other faiths, others suggest that in fact only *amritdhāri* Sikhs should be deemed eligible for the *anand kāraj*.

OTHER DIASPORA DEVELOPMENTS

PUNJAB POLITICS

Given Sikhs' understanding of the indivisibility of *mīrī* and *pīrī* (temporal and spiritual authority), gurdwaras have played their part in diaspora Sikhs' political engagement. Together with the local challenges to the right to bear the *kirpān* or wear the turban, Punjab's politics too has provided successive rallying points for diaspora Sikhs. So, in the early 2020s, many overseas

Sikhs identified with the Punjabi farmers' movement.[12] Engagement with political issues in India has resulted in support for organizations such as (in the 1980s in the United Kingdom) the Babbar Khalsa and the International Sikh Youth Federation. Other UK-based organizations are the Sikh Federation (UK), the Sikh Council, the British Sikh Consultative Forum, and the Network of Sikh Organisations.

In the present century, media attention is sporadically drawn to the activity of a minority of overseas Sikhs, especially in Canada, in support of establishing a separate Sikh state of Khalistan, a political cause that also has some support among Sikhs in the United Kingdom and elsewhere.

Sikhs in Canada and the United Kingdom have protested increasingly about being regarded as potential terrorists on the basis of some overseas Sikhs' support for the creation of Khalistan. In 2023, in the United Kingdom, for example, Sikh organizations were quick to respond to the "Colin Bloom Faith Report" in which, together with commendation of the contribution of the Sikh majority to British society, attention was drawn to the activity of extremist groups. This included the divisive output of some Sikh broadcasting channels.

MEDIA

At the time of writing, specifically Sikh television companies include Sangat TV, Sikh Channel, and Panjab Broadcasting Channel. Diaspora media had begun over 100 years earlier with, for example, Punjabi print periodicals that were published in Vancouver from 1907, in Malaya from 1935, and in the United Kingdom from 1965 or earlier.

Lilly Singh became the first person of Indian and South Asian descent and openly bisexual person to host an American broadcast major network talk show. *A Little Late with Lilly Singh* was aired on NBC from 2019 to 2021.

SPORT

In the world of sport, Monty Panesar (Mudhsuden Singh Panesar) came to prominence as an England cricketer. Fauja Singh

(b. 1911) became well known for running marathons in his late 80s: he ran marathons in Hong Kong and London, continuing to run when he was over 100. (At the time of writing, he is 114 years old.) Another marathon runner, Preet Kaur (Captain Harpreet Kaur Chandi, also known as "Polar Preet"), made history as a woman of color in January 2022 by completing a solo expedition across Antarctica to the South Pole and then, a year later, by recording the longest ever solo, unsupported polar expedition. Kabaḍḍi tournaments are enthusiastically supported in the United Kingdom, kabaḍḍi being a popular contact team sport in South Asia. At the same time, there are Sikh players in a growing number of UK football teams.

EDUCATION

Throughout the worldwide diaspora, Sikhs express concern about the erosion of Punjabi language and Sikh religion and culture. Partly for this reason Khalsa schools have been established in the United Kingdom, United States, Canada, Singapore, Malaysia, Indonesia, and Thailand to provide a grounding in the Sikh tradition together with a full academic curriculum. By 2024 there were 13 state-funded Sikh schools in the United Kingdom. Nonetheless, the vast majority of young Sikhs are educated in mainstream schools and rely on their homes and gurdwaras to learn to speak Punjabi, to read Gurmukhi, and hone their skills in *shabad kīrtan* and Sikh martial arts. Many have the opportunity to participate in youth camps in the United Kingdom, mainland Europe, Canada, Malaysia, and the United States. At the same time the internet facilitates peer-to-peer sharing and discussion of all aspects of Sikh experience. Moreover, the problem of younger generations not understanding the Guru Granth Sahib is in part addressed in gurdwaras by using screens to display an English translation of the scriptural passages spoken and sung during worship.

Sikh studies is well established in higher education in several countries – especially in the United States and Canada. At the time of writing, Sikh studies research and teaching in higher education in the United Kingdom is carried out across several university departments, such as religious studies, but the subject has not had the benefit of endowed Sikh chairs in universities despite the Sikh population being of a similar size to that in the United States.

PHILANTHROPY

Diaspora Sikhs' strongly continuing relationship with Punjab is evident in many ways, including overseas Sikhs' philanthropy.[13] As early as 1923 Sikhs from Stockton, United States founded Khalsa Middle School in Khan Khana near Shaheed Bhagat Singh Nagar (previously known as Nawanshahr) in Punjab. Individual Sikhs and hometown or village associations in the diaspora fund not only educational institutions but also gurdwaras, hospitals, dispensaries and eye camps, renewable energy programs, and infrastructure such as water treatment and sewerage, plus rural development projects.[14] East African Sikhs have made donations for Ramgarhia colleges in Punjab and one project of the Birmingham (UK)-based Guru Nanak Nishkam Sewak Jatha was regilding Harmandar Sahib.

India's Punjab state is being viewed as a holy land for visits to historical gurdwaras. Moreover, for Sikhs whose passports are not Indian, visits to Nankana Sahib, Panja Sahib, and Pakistan's other Sikh historical sites are easier than for Indian nationals.

SANTS

Indian Punjab is also the base of *sant*s, charismatic religious preachers whose followers in due course set up gurdwaras. In the United Kingdom and North America some "*sant* gurdwaras" have become models of religious worship, with their strong emphasis on *nām simran* and *kīrtan* and their strict codes of religious discipline. Some *sant*s are part of a particular succession, a prominent example being the *sant*s claiming spiritual descent from Baba Nand Singh (1870–1943) of Nanaksar near Jagraon in Punjab.[15] Nanaksar gurdwaras are to be found in Coventry, Smethwick, and other places in the British Midlands, as well as in British Columbia, Ontario, Fresno, California, and Houston, Texas. To give another itinerant *sant*s' example, Sant Teja Singh (1877–1965) visited gurdwaras in California and British Columbia during 1908–1911 and administered *amrit*.

Sant Ishar Singh Rarewale (1905–1975) visited the United Kingdom to preach and died there in 1975. The Birmingham (UK)-based Guru Nanak Nishkam Sewak Jatha originated with Sant Puran Singh (1898–1983), not in India but in Kericho, Kenya and now, led by Bhai Mohinder Singh, implements major initiatives within the Sikh community and beyond.[16] In 1976 Sant Puran Singh lent his support to the successful campaign for turban-wearing Sikh motorcyclists to be exempted by United Kingdom law from the requirement to wear crash helmets.

Unusually, the activity of one now discredited United States–based *sant*, Harbhajan Singh Puri (1929–2004), a controversial teacher of kundalini yoga, resulted in the adoption of Sikh faith by several thousand Western followers. Distinctively, both men and women adherents of his organization, 3HO (Healthy, Happy, Holy Organization), and the associated Sikh Dharma of the Western Hemisphere, wear white turbans and use the surname "Khalsa."

LANGAR AND SEVĀ

Meanwhile the *langar* tradition's impetus to share food with the hungry now reaches far beyond gurdwara premises, and *sevā* has assumed a higher international profile through the hunger and emergency relief provided unstintingly by a growing number of organizations such as Khalsa Aid, United Sikhs, and (in the United Kingdom) Langar Aid and the Sikh Empowerment Voluntary Association. Examples of *sevā*: Canadian Sikh Council, Dasvandh Network, EcoSikh, Ensaaf, the Jakara Movement, Kaur Foundation, Kaurs United, Khoj Gurbani, Sikh Feminist Research Institute, Sikh American Legal Defense and Education Fund, Sikh Coalition, Sikh Family Center, Sikh Helpline Australia, Sikh Research Institute, Sikh Women, Sikh Women Now, Sikh Youth Federation, Sikhcess, Sikhlens, Surat Initiative, United Nations–affiliated United Sikhs, and World Sikh Organization of Canada. All are dedicated to the realization of civil and human rights for all people and the guardianship of the earth.

The United Kingdom–based charity Khalsa Aid International (founded in 1999) has brought timely support to victims of wars and natural disasters worldwide – for instance, in Kosovo in

1999; for Yazidi refugees on the Iraq border in 2014; for Rohingya Muslim refugees in Bangladesh in 2017; and for victims of the Nepal earthquake and an Australian cyclone in 2015, as well as the floods in Kerala in 2018. In Australia, relief came from a local *sevā* organization, Turbans for Australia. Other local Sikh charities, based in different countries, brought relief during the COVID-19 pandemic and after acts of terrorism. In December 2016, Zero Hunger with Langar started serving nutritious food daily at places of education across southern Malawi. Far beyond countries with settled Sikh populations, Sikhs are becoming known for their faithful, timely dedication to serving humanity.

LITERATURE, ART, AND FILM

Sikh servicemen in the two World Wars are the subject of *Across the Black Waters* (1939) by Indian novelist Mulk Raj Anand and *The English Patient* (1994) by Canadian Sri Lankan novelist Michael Ondaatje. Fictional diaspora Sikhs in novels include an early Sikh settler in Australia in David Martin's *The Man in the Red Turban* (1979) and the remarkable sleuth Inspector Singh in Singaporean author Shamini Flint's detective novels. After the best-selling novelist J.K. Rowling's Harry Potter series was completed, a Sikh family – and particularly Dr. Parminder Jawanda and her daughter Sukhvinder – were central to her first novel for adults, *The Casual Vacancy* (2012). Rowling's portrayal is sympathetic, but the SGPC requested the removal of offensive remarks that a bully made about Sukhvinder.

Sikhs are also finding their way into public sculpture: in sculptor Paul Day's "The Meeting Place" in St Pancras railway station in London, the eagle-eyed will find, in relief, around the base of the installation, a turbaned Sikh among the men depicted laying railway sleepers. In Cardiff's Central Square, a Sikh boy wearing a *patkā* (covering for his hair) figures in Eve Shepherd's statue of Wales's first Black headteacher.

In 1996 *The English Patient* appeared as a film directed by Anthony Minghella. In 2017 a historical drama film, *The Black Prince*, was made by Indian-born British actor, writer, director, and producer Kavi Raz. (The exiled Duleep Singh had acquired the nickname "Black Prince of Perthshire" when he was in Scotland.) Other non-Sikh directors have also taken up the subject of Sikhs overseas. Thus, in *Continuous Journey* (2004), Ali Kazami documents the 1914 voyage of the Japanese steamship *Komagata Maru* chartered by Sikh businessman Gurdit Singh to transport Indian immigrants over to Canada, while Jayasri Majumdar Hart's *Roots in the Sand* is a multi-generational documentary film on the trials and triumphs of the earliest Punjabi immigrants (mostly Sikh men) who settled in Southern California's Imperial Valley.

So much for the presence of diaspora Sikhs in works by non-Sikhs. In its wider coverage of Sikhs and the arts more generally, chapter 6 is a taster of the creative ferment of diaspora Sikh writers and artists, engaging with their complex experience as South Asians of Sikh heritage.

NOTES

1 See Darshan Singh Tatla, *The Sikh Diaspora: The Search for Statehood* (London: UCL Press, 1999) for arguments for and against using this term.
2 Martin Baumann, "Migration, Diaspora, and Religion," in *The Routledge Handbook of Transregional Studies*, ed. Matthias Middell (London: Routledge, 2019), 456–563.
3 Steven Vertovec, "Three Meanings of 'Diaspora,' Exemplified among South Asian Religions," *Diaspora: A Journal of Transnational Studies* 6, no. 3 (1997): 277–299.
4 Darshan Singh Tatla, *The Sikh Diaspora: The Search for Statehood* (London: UCL Press, 2006).
5 See "Afghanistan's Last Sikhs in a Dilemma: To Stay or Leave," *Al Jazeera*, January 20, 2022, https://www.aljazeera.com/news/2022/1/20/stay-or-go-dilemma-facing-last-afghanistan-sikhs.
6 For China, see Ka-Kin Cheuk, "China Including Hong Kong," in *Brill's Encyclopedia of Sikhism, vol. 1*, ed. Knut A. Jacobsen, Gurinder Singh Mann, Kristina Myrvold, and Eleanor Nesbitt (Leiden: Brill, 2017), 473–479.
7 Karen Leonard, *Making Ethnic Choices: California's Punjabi Mexican Americans* (Philadelphia: Temple University Press, 1994).
8 The voyage of the *Komagata Maru* is studied by Hugh J.W. Johnston, *The Voyage of the Komagata Maru: The Sikh Challenge to Canada's Colour Bar* (Chicago: Chicago University Press [1979] 2014).
9 See Gurharpal Singh and Darshan Singh Tatla, *Sikhs in Britain: The Making of a Community* (London: Zed, 2006).

10 For continental Europe, see Eleanor Nesbitt, "Sikhs in Mainland Europe," in *The Sikh World*, ed. Arvind-pal Singh Mandair and Pashaura Singh (London: Routledge, 2023), 160–170.
11 On classes in the gurdwara, see Eleanor Nesbitt, *The Religious Lives of Sikh Children: A Coventry Based Study* (Leeds: Department of Theology and Religious Studies, University of Leeds, 2000), 143–150.
12 See Shinder S. Thandi, "*Mera Pind, Mera Sabhyachar, Mera Virsa*: Understanding Sikh Diaspora Support for the Punjab Kisan Morcha," in *Agrarian Reform and Farmer Resistance in Punjab: Mobilization and Resistance*, ed. Shinder S. Thandi (New Delhi: Routledge, 2022).
13 For philanthropy, see Verne A. Dusenbery and Darshan S. Tatla, *Sikh Diaspora Philanthropy in Punjab: Global Giving for Local Good* (New Delhi: Oxford University Press, 2006).
14 Shinder S. Thandi, "Diasporas and Development: Can Diaspora Finance and Philanthropy Deliver Human Development in Punjab?" in *Globalization and Change: Perspectives from Punjab Essays in Honour of Sucha Singh Gill*, ed. Ranjit S. Ghuman and Jaswinder S. Brar (Jaipur: Rawat Publications, 2010), 366–386.
15 For Nanaksar, see Eleanor Nesbitt, "Nanaksar," in *Brill's Encyclopedia of Sikhism, vol. 1*, ed. Knut A. Jacobsen, Gurinder Singh Mann, Kristina Myrvold, and Eleanor Nesbitt (Leiden: Brill, 2017), 380–385.
16 Opinderjit Kaur Takhar, "Guru Nanak Nishkam Sewak Jatha," in *Brill's Encyclopedia of Sikhism, vol. 1*, ed. Knut A. Jacobsen, Gurinder Singh Mann, Kristina Myrvold, and Eleanor Nesbitt (Leiden: Brill, 2017), 394–396.

REFERENCES AND FURTHER READING

Cheuk, Ka Kin. "China Including Hong Kong." In *Brill's Encyclopedia of Sikhism, vol. 1*, edited by Knut Jacobsen, Gurinder Singh Mann, Kristina Myrvold, and Eleanor Nesbitt, 473–479. Leiden: Brill, 2017.

Johnston, Hugh J. M. *The Voyage of the Komagata Maru: The Sikh Challenge to Canada's Colour Bar*. Chicago: University of Chicago Press, [1979] 2014.

Leonard, Karen. *Making Ethnic Choices: California's Punjabi Mexican Americans*. Philadelphia: Temple University Press, 1994.

Nesbitt, Eleanor. "Sikhs in Mainland Europe." In *The Sikh World*, edited by Arvind-pal Singh Mandair and Pashaura Singh, 160–170. London: Routledge, 2023.

Nesbitt, Eleanor. *The Religious Lives of Sikh Children: A Coventry Based Study*. Leeds: Department of Theology and Religious Studies, University of Leeds, 2000.

Singh, Gurharpal, and Darshan Singh Tatla. *Sikhs in Britain: The Making of a Community*. London: Zed, 2006.

Singh, Nikky-Guninder Kaur. "My Dinner in Calgary: Sikh Diaspora in the Making." In *Sikh Diaspora: Theory, Agency, and Experience*, edited by Michael Hawley, 89–101. Leiden: Brill, 2013.

Tatla, Darshan Singh. *The Sikh Diaspora: The Search for Statehood*. London: UCL Press, 1999.

6

ART AND LITERATURE

INTRODUCTION

"For the Sikhs, by the Sikhs, and about the Sikhs," Sikh art includes sacred and secular works, by Sikhs and non-Sikhs, depicting Sikh themes. However, unlike the art of the Buddhists, Jains, Hindus, Muslims, and Christians from the Indian subcontinent, Sikh art is only now beginning to gain attention. Art is also generally neglected in the study of religion; even though "religion," especially another's, can be daunting, art has no boundaries. As the Russian painter and art theorist Wassily Kandinsky famously said, art is the power essential for the raising of the "spiritual triangle."[1]

The tercentenary celebrations of the founding of the Khalsa in 1999 generated visual and literary creations and scholarly conferences, as did the fourth centennial of the Guru Granth Sahib in 2004, and the 550th birth celebrations of Guru Nanak in 2019. Galleries worldwide display illustrations of the ten Gurus, scriptural manuscripts, jewelry, coins, weapons, sculptures, textiles, and objects in gold, silver, and copper in all their regional and stylistic variations. Sikh patrons have established permanent galleries – for instance, in North America, the Kapany Gallery of Sikh Art at the Asian Art Museum in San Francisco, the Khanuja Sikh Art Gallery at the Phoenix Art Museum, and the Montreal Museum of Fine Arts in its Arts of One World wing. Objects from the Toor Collection of Sikh Art in the United Kingdom have been exhibited at major global institutions.

DOI: 10.4324/9781003359210-6

SCRIPTURAL MANUSCRIPTS

Illuminated and illustrated manuscripts are found from Kabul in the west to Patna in the East.[2] At this stage of research, not much is known about their artists, their scribes, or their patrons. Jeevan Deol, a pioneer in this field, distinguishes three types of manuscripts: (1) early manuscripts with *nisāns* – from the Persian for "sign" or "emblem," (2) others with illumination or floral adornment, and (3) illustrated manuscripts. The *nisāns* generally consist of *mūl mantar* purportedly written in the Guru's own hand on a fragment of paper. Devotees placed these *nisāns* in their sacred volume as a precious token of the Guru's blessing. Most manuscripts bearing *nisāns* date from the 17th century, and most extant *nisāns* are attributed to the ninth and tenth Gurus.[3]

Manuscripts of the second genre contain abstract geometric patterns reminiscent of Persian works. Simple cursive lettering gives way to a highly ornamental script.[4] The Persian sunburst (*shamsa*), the divine light (*nur* of the holy Qur'an), and the highly ornate Islamicate blue and gold lettering (*unvan*) appear in Sikh sacred volumes from the 17th to the mid-19th century. These show that the Sikh volumes were a product of professional book illuminators, trained in illustrating Arabic and Persian manuscripts. Like the scriptural verses, their intricate designs with tendrils, leaves, buds, and flowers embody organic life and rhythm. Under Maharaja Ranjit Singh, gold was used extensively in writing and illuminating texts. Reputedly, the most lavish scriptural volume was created for the maharaja in an ink mixed with gold, diamonds, and emeralds.

Manuscripts with figural decoration constitute the third category. The adornment of Guru Granth Sahib manuscripts changed largely due to the mid-18th-century arrival of Kashmiri painters and scribes in Punjab. The collapse of Mughal sovereignty quickened artists' dispersal across North India. Some were unemployed itinerants from the Pahari schools or the Mughal ateliers and, during winters, offered their talents to clients in the plains, while others worked for years for a single patron. In their decorative style and color selection, the Kashmiri artists' illuminations differ from the earlier Islamicate ones. They began to illustrate Guru

Granth Sahib manuscripts with portraits of the ten Gurus on the main text's opening folio. Sometimes the Gurus appear with their families, sometimes (more controversially) with Indic deities. In the late 19th century, the printing press took over the production of scriptural copies, and now the only reminders of a lost art are the vines, flowers, and geometric borders in modern volumes.

THE *JANAMSĀKHĪS*

As discussed in chapter 1, soon after Guru Nanak's lifetime, *sākhīs* (witnessed stories) about his birth (*janam*) and life began to circulate orally, in writing, and in illustrations. They commemorate Guru Nanak and his message rather than being strictly factual, and they provide a stage for interpreting his teachings, so creating a symbiosis between his biography and his compositions. As patrons from Sikh centers in the Punjab and beyond commissioned local writers and artists, numerous *janamsākhīs* were produced in different regions at different periods. These include the Bala, Miharban, Adi, and Puratan *janamsākhīs*.

The earliest extant illustrated *janamsākhīs* listed are dated to 1658, 1724, and 1733.[5] Later *janamsākhīs* include those produced by the Nainsukh family of artists in Guler, now in the Government Museum in Chandigarh, and the Kapany Unbound Set at the Asian Arts Museum in San Francisco. *Janamsākhī* illustrations exemplify multiple artistic styles. Art historians have discovered that templates with rough sketches of the Guru's biography were used by different groups of painters and scribes, and so manuscripts from diverse regions contain similar depictions of particular scenes. The *B-40 Janamsākhī* stands out for providing historical documentation – date, patron, scribe, and artist. Visual images and verbal narratives along with scriptural poetry inscribed in vernacular Punjabi combine, so making Guru Nanak, his message and poetry accessible.

The Unbound Kapany Collection contains four paintings of Guru Nanak's wedding. In pinks, yellows, oranges, and golden brown, one sees a variety of musical instruments, the procession of the groom's party to the bride's home, the reception by the bride's family, the wedding, and the departure of the bride with the groom from her natal home. The wedding procession registers a confident groom riding a white horse amid merry-making. The couple's matching attires create a warm intimacy. Even the plume on her head ornament matches his.[6] Sikh spectators may recall the scriptural verse, "*ek joti dūi murtī* – one light, two bodies" (GGS: 788).

THE TEN GURUS

Early portraits of the Sikh Gurus are in the courtly Mughal style, developed under Emperor Akbar and refined under his son Jahangir and grandson Shah Jahan. Its foundations are traceable to Sayyid Ali and Abdus Samad, artists from Iran who reached India—thanks to the Mughal emperor Humayun. Their integrating of local Hindu, Jain, and Buddhist styles shaped the distinct style of "Mughal" art. Under successive Mughal rulers, artists from the Punjab plains and the Pahari areas learned the Mughal style of painting. Consequently, when they portrayed the Sikh Gurus, their physical features, as well as their outfits, turbans, and poses resembled Mughal aristocrats. Some works, produced at flourishing art centers such as Guler and Kangra, have intricate patterns and technical finesse characteristic of Mughal miniatures. The collection at Gurdwara Ram Rai, Dehra Dun provides Sikh art's earliest examples of portraiture. These paintings, commissioned by Ram Rai (b. 1646), the elder son of Guru Har Rai (Nanak 7), remained in his descendants' custody. Thereafter, portraits of the ten Gurus appear in the early 18th century. The Gurus are briefly identified in Persian, Gurmukhi, or Devanagari scripts. Guru Nanak is the most conspicuous figure, and his four successor Gurus are modeled on his image, whereas Guru Hargobind is portrayed in royal regalia, wearing an aigrette on his turban, carrying weapons, riding horses, and usually sporting a falcon on a gloved hand. The next three Gurus replicate the style of the first five.

The pageantry returns dramatically with Guru Gobind Singh, popularly called (like the emperors of Iran) *Shāh-i-Shāhān*, meaning "King of Kings." Wearing precious jewels, elegant shoes, and a towering aigrette in his turban, he rides spirited stallions with jeweled harnesses and carries a bow across his shoulder, a quiver of arrows on one side, a sword on the other, and a dagger in his waistband. Hunting dogs cavort alongside his stallion. A majestic parasol carried by his attendant augments his imperial glory. We see the hero extolled in folk songs with a white falcon, riding a blue horse and wearing a royal aigrette.

Guru Gobind Singh was a great poet and patron of the arts. In Paunta, the town he founded by the river Jamuna, poets from different religious backgrounds gathered, and the Guru employed 52 poets permanently. Among them was Nand Lal Goya who was born in Ghazni, Afghanistan and wrote praises of the Gurus and the mystery of the Divine in beautiful Persian works such as the *Ganjnāmā* and *Zindagīnāmā*.

Poetry symposia were held, and poetry was Guru Gobind Singh's own medium to reorient his community. He composed in invigorating meters. His images and paradoxes would stretch their imagination, and his themes from ancient Indian epics and mythology would evoke martial fervor. Although the actual authorship and the content of parts of the 1,428-paged Dasam Granth that is attributed to him remain controversial, the *Jāp, Akāl Ustati, Bicitra Nāṭak, Caṇḍī Caritra, Caṇḍī dī Vār, Shabad Hazāre*, and *Giān Prabodh* are generally revered by Sikhs as Guru Gobind Singh's own compositions rather than those of poets in his entourage. With its abundance of divine attributes, his popularly recited *Jāp* carries forward the first Guru's *Japji* at breathtaking speed.

After Guru Gobind Singh's demise in 1708, Sikhs went through a tumultuous time (see chapter 2). One new literary genre that developed was the *rahitnāmā* – that is, codes regulating Sikh practice and custom. They were terse, apophthegmatic, and hortatory in style, often reversing the Gurus' more progressive message. For instance, the *Chaupā Singh Rahitnāmā* dictates a Sikh woman's primary mode of religiosity as her worship of her husband: she is to "know her husband as god – *apne bharte nū kartā jānai*"; she is to "keep fasts for the sake of her husband – *patibrat rakhe*."[7] Such prescriptions seem inconsistent with the egalitarian tone struck by Guru Nanak. The series ended with the 1950 publication of *Sikh Rahit Maryādā*, which continues to be the authoritative Sikh code of conduct for men and women.

Some historical works also emerged during the 18th century. They belong to the genre of *Gurbilās* literature (*guru* + *bilās* = splendor of the Guru), narrative poetry exalting the Gurus' heroic fight for justice. The focus of Kavi Sohan's *Gurbilās Chhevin Pātshāhī* is Guru Hargobind, and both Sukha Singh in *Gurbilās Dasvin Pātshāhī* and Koer Singh in *Gurbilās Pātshāhī 10* showcase Guru Gobind Singh. Sainpati's *Sri Gur Sobhā* (Radiance of the Guru) also depicts his life and is especially valuable for describing his founding of the Khalsa.[8]

SIKH EMPIRE

Art flourished in the empire of Maharaja Ranjit Singh (r. 1799–1839). Ranjit Singh patronized Persian, Hindi, and Punjabi scholars and poets, and the construction of sacred places and objects for his Muslim, Hindu, and Sikh subjects alike. He had little formal education but fostered the circulation of literature. Educational centers affiliated with mosques, temples, and gurdwaras received grants; works in the Gurmukhi, Persian, and Devanagari scripts were equally supported.

The maharaja's chronicler and diplomatic representative Sohan Lal Suri composed the monumental *Umdāt-ut-Tawārīkh* in Persian, covering Sikh history from the birth of Guru Nanak in 1469 to the British annexation of Punjab in 1849. Amar Nath, Bute Shah, Khushwaqt Rai, and Kanhaiya Lal also recorded Punjab and Sikh history. Along with the state language of Persian, the maharaja promoted Punjabi literature. The Puranas, Ramayana, and Bhagavad Gita were translated from Sanskrit into Punjabi. Muslim poets Hashim Shah, Ahmad Yar, and Qadir Yar produced highly sophisticated works in Punjabi.

Painting, architecture, jewelry, weaponry, coinage, and crafts received patronage. Forts, palaces, gurdwaras, mosques, and temples were built; luxurious tents, canopies, caparisons, and large woolen shawls which could slip through a tiny ring were created. Highlights include the embellishment of the Golden Temple, the bejeweled canopy for the Guru Granth, the "golden volume" presented to the Gurdwara at Nanded in Maharashtra, the gold throne made by Hafez Muhammad Multani, and fine jewelry. Transcending religious boundaries, Ranjit Singh's benefactions included silver doors for goddess Kali's temple and a costly manuscript copy of the holy Qur'an. Like Banda Bahadur (see chapter 2), Ranjit Singh issued coins in the name of the Gurus, so justifying his own rule. Persian couplets inscribed on gold mohur and silver rupee coins include

> Glory to the cooking pot (*degh*) and the sword (*tegh*), victory without delay!
> Obtained from Nanak, Guru Gobind Singh.[9]

While celebrating the spiritual transmission from the first to the tenth Guru, Sikh victory is here idealized in the image of the *degh* (cooking pot) – food from the common kitchen so that nobody would go hungry, and *tegh* (sword) – freedom in the fight against political, religious, and racial oppression. The early coins were inscribed in Persian, though later on, Gurmukhi and Devanagari were used, often with the words, "*Gurū Nānakjī*" and "*Akāl Sahāī*" (Timeless One is the Protector).

Centers such as Lahore, Amritsar, Srinagar, Multan, and Sialkot produced artifacts for the maharaja and his court. For their residences, aristocrats and Europeans at his court commissioned architects, craftsmen, and artists in many media – fresco, ivory, wood, stucco, embossed gold, inlaid mosaic, and mirror work. Artists in the Sikh school of painting included Imam Baksh, Kapur Singh, Kehar Singh, Kishan Singh, and Bishan Singh. A bronze bust of Ranjit Singh, installed in 2016 in Saint-Tropez, the birthplace of his French army general Jean-François Allard, fittingly commemorates his intercultural relationships.

THE GOLDEN TEMPLE

Ranjit Singh's outstanding accomplishment was commissioning Muslim architects, masons, wood-carvers, and other craftsmen to refurbish Amritsar's Harmandar as the Golden Temple. Yar Mohommad Khan Mistri was the technical expert for the gold plating.

Approached by a causeway bordered by marble balustrades, the Golden Temple rises from the sacred pool. Its marble exterior is inlaid with lapis lazuli, onyx, and other semiprecious stones in the *pietra dura* technique. Its upper part is covered with plates of gilded copper that shimmer in the surrounding waters. The interior of its second storey, with walls and ceiling sparkling with mirrors and colored glass, opens up in the center to reveal the Guru Granth Sahib enshrined on the ground floor. Ranjit Singh gifted its canopy, studded with pearls and jewels. In borders around the walls, deer, lions, cobras, and elephants hold flower vases and fruits.

WESTERN REPRESENTATIONS

The Golden Temple's beauty is captured by the American artist John Edwin Lord Weeks (1849–1903):

> From the border of the tank, which lies in the afternoon shadow, the Golden Temple gives one the impression of a glittering jewel, or of some rare old Byzantine casket wrought in enamel and studded with gems. Small and compact, glowing with colour and scintillating with light, its mirrored image reaching far down into the purple depths of reflected sky, it has at first sight a glamour of unreality, like an opium vision of De Quincey, or the "pleasure dome of Kubla Khan."[10]

Weeks painted the Golden Temple in the picturesque genre with its typical chiaroscuro effect. In the distance the Sikh shrine emerges in dazzling light reflected in the glowing waters, but the forefront is shadowy. Sikhs and their historical gurdwaras, especially Harmandar Sahib, drew the attention of many Western artists. The British artist William Carpenter's watercolors display both the outside and the interior. In his painting (in the V&A, London) of the inner sanctum, the Guru Granth Sahib rests on cushions while musicians are playing the *tānpurā* (typically a four-stringed instrument) and *tablā*s (drums). One of the earliest and largest panoramic views of the Golden Temple in watercolors is by Major Charles Herbert. A watercolor by William Simpson (1864) presents a part of the Golden Temple complex with the Akal Bunga (Timeless House – i.e., Akāl Takht) in the backdrop and the Sikh flag fluttering.

Among the women artists, Emily Eden is probably the best known. She and her sister had come to Punjab in December 1838 with their brother, who had been appointed India's governor general. Eden described their visit to the Golden Temple, escorted by the maharaja himself. A few years later, watercolors painted by Matilda Saunders show the Golden Temple and other well-known shrines (Toor Collection). Watercolors by Charlotte Canning, the wife of India's first viceroy, offer almost aerial views of the Golden Temple and of Lahore's Shalimar Gardens, Mughal gardens beloved by Ranjit Singh. Marianne North's medium was oil paints. She too conveyed the beauty of the Golden Temple and other locations in Amritsar and Lahore.[11]

Emily Eden also captured the wild appearance of Akali warriors and the splendor of the Sikh court, the debonair Sikh princes and nobles, their dazzling costumes and ornamented horses. In her watercolor of Maharaja Ranjit Singh, sitting comfortably, with one foot tucked under him in a chair, he wears a plain red outfit and simple headwear. Her paintings are displayed in the Victoria Memorial Hall in Kolkata.

On a canvas that dominated the Vienna exhibition, the Hungarian artist August Schoefft (1809–1888) painted *The Court of Lahore*. Along with the maharaja's family, numerous employees can be identified. Schoefft also painted the maharaja in the presence of the Guru Granth Sahib at the Golden Temple. With the houses and minarets of the city of Amritsar in the background, the Golden Temple rises from the waters, and in the foreground, we see him listening respectfully to the scripture in the open air. Schoefft's oil painting illustrates the literary testimony of an English visitor that "the Granth was constantly read to him,"[12] while other artists portrayed him sitting grandly in his court or horse riding.

Schoefft's portrait of Ranjit Singh's son and successor, Maharaja Sher Singh, shows him bejeweled, seated on his father's golden throne, holding an upright sword,[13] probably the first Sikh to be pictured with his beard tied. Schoefft also painted Sher Singh surrounded by his council in the Lahore Fort and the young prince Duleep Singh dressed in bright red and gold, with Punjabi golden embroidered shoes, and a jeweled sword in his hand, seated, oddly, on a tree trunk.[14]

WOMEN SUBJECTS

Sikh women are seldom subjects of Sikh art. However, the court artist Kehar Singh sketched Rani Sada Kaur (1762–1832), Ranjit Singh's influential mother-in-law, and Schoefft painted Maharani Jindan, the regent of the Sikh empire from 1843 until 1846, sitting confidently on a cushion, resting against a pillow with her head held high (Princess Bamba Collection, Lahore, Pakistan). The Kapany Collection includes her famous portrait by George Richmond (1863), and she is also the probable subject of a late 19th-century portrayal (exuding authority and intelligence) from the Jaipur school of painting.[15]

Ten years after the death of Maharaja Ranjit Singh, the British annexed the Punjab. In 1875 the Mayo School of Arts was established in Lahore with John Lockwood Kipling as principal.

EARLY COLONIAL PERIOD

Three-dimensional perspective was introduced, and painting in oil became common practice. The earlier Mughal naturalism and Pahari lyricism combined with Western realism added a new dimension to the Sikh school of painting.

PATIALA ON THE ART MAP

Maharaja Narinder Singh (1824–1862) made his princely state of Patiala a cultural hub for painters, poets, musicians, builders, craftsmen, and gardeners from different religious backgrounds and different parts of North India. Eminent classical singers were invited to the court, and the Patiala *gharānā* of Hindustani music acquired much fame. Eminent artists from Jaipur, the Pahari regions, and the Mughal court migrated to Patiala to work on the extensive murals for his forts, palaces, and shrines. Maharaja Narinder Singh's promotion of the arts provided a model for his successors and for the rulers of Nabha, Kapurthala, Faridkot, and Jind. Paintings of the Sikh Gurus, illustrated manuscripts, rich murals, royal portraits, and works capturing the unsung "lower" segment of society were produced all over the Sikh kingdoms. Kishan Singh, Bishan Singh, and

Kapur Singh were popular Sikh artists. They tried to reproduce the lost glory of the Sikh raj and record their own situation realistically in gouache, watercolor, and oils.

ARCHITECT BHAI RAM SINGH

Bhai Ram Singh (1857–1916) belonged to the Ramgarhia community, known for its distinctive contributions to Sikh art and architecture. As Lockwood Kipling's one-time star student at the Mayo School of Arts, he was later appointed as a teacher there and eventually as the principal. Ram Singh combined Gothic and neoclassical architectural styles with Hindu, Mughal, and other Indo-Islamic designs for the Mayo School of Art, the Governor's House in Simla, the Lahore Museum, Aitchison College, Punjab University, Albert Victor Hospital, Islamia College Peshawar, and the Khalsa College in Amritsar. He received many awards and was commissioned by Queen Victoria to design the Durbar Room at Osborne House, her summer residence on the Isle of Wight. With its spread of floral patterns on the ceiling, its honeycomb vaulting, overhanging balconies in carved teak wood, and ornate peacock above the fireplace, the Durbar Room brought India to the empress of India.

LATER COLONIAL PERIOD

ARTISTS

In the first half of the 20th century Thakur Singh (1899–1976), initially a stage artist in Bombay, soon became the state artist for several maharajas. His output included celebrity portraits, natural landscapes, and monuments including the Golden Temple. He later established the Thakur Singh School of Arts in Amritsar whose members subsequently played an important role in the creation of the Central Sikh Museum at the Golden Temple.

Sobha Singh (1901–1986) witnessed human violence during his army service and produced paintings expressive of peace and love, including images of immortal lovers from the Punjabi folk romances of Heer-Ranjha, Sassi-Punnu, and Sohni-Mahival. His popular masterpiece is a portrait of Guru Nanak, which is now imprinted in the Sikh imagination. The Guru's face with his white beard is tenderly bent, his turban and robe are a soft yellow, his eyes brim with spirituality, and his hand is raised in benediction. Ubiquitous prints of this painting serve as a prime marker of a Sikh home.

Born in Budapest, Amrita Sher-Gil (1913–1941) is the most celebrated artist of modern Indian painting. Her aristocratic Sikh photographer father had fallen in love with Hungary's noted opera singer who accompanied Princess Bamba Jindan (one of Maharaja Duleep Singh's daughters) during her visit to the Punjab. Sher-Gil had trained at the École des Beaux-Arts in Paris. Catholic and Jewish from her mother's side, she inherited the Sikh tradition from her father. Captivated by the cave paintings at Ajanta, she denounced the Orientalized romanticism dominating the Indian art scene and set out to bring an existentialist realism to Indian painting. Sher-Gil explored the lives of the poor Indian masses in colonial India, aiming "to paint those silent images of infinite submission and patience . . . to a plane which transcends."[16] Her works have been declared national treasures: stamps reproducing her paintings were issued. Her letters were adapted into a play, and UNESCO declared her birth centennial as the international year of Amrita Sher-Gil. *The Musicians* (1940) depicts three Sikh musicians in white turbans against a deep green background seated closely together on a Punjabi handwoven cotton rug (*durri*) with geometric designs. This is her only painting of a specifically Sikh scene, a *kīrtan* performance, although *The Ancient Storyteller* (painted the same year) also evokes the *janamsākhī* genre and a Nanak-like figure.[17]

WRITERS

After the annexation of the Punjab in 1849, the rich heterogeneous linguistic world of precolonial Punjab — where Punjabi language was common to Muslims, Hindus, and Sikhs — was reduced to Urdu for the Muslims, Hindi for Hindus, and Punjabi for the Sikhs. In a wide range of literary styles, writers like the Sikh Bhai Vir Singh (1872–1957), Hindu Dhani Ram Chatrik (1876–1954), and Muslim Firoz Din Sharaf (1898–1955) brought a revolutionary transformation in the Punjabi language.

Bhai Vir Singh (1872–1957) was the leading figure in the Singh Sabha, the Sikh renaissance movement, which aspired to align Punjabi culture with the principles of the Sikh Gurus. Under the British Raj, Christian missions and English schools and colleges brought the Punjab into the orbit of a new literary consciousness. Ironically, this introduction to Western ideologies fostered the development of indigenous cultural traditions and vernacular Punjabi literature. Writers responded to the challenges of rapid social and cultural change. Bhai Vir Singh published eight collections of poetry, four novels, a play, five biographies, and nine major texts that he meticulously annotated – while keeping up with his journalism. His writing can be summed up as an exposition of the Guru Granth Sahib.

Imaginative works have a way of reaching deep into the psyche of their readers, so in order to restore the ethical values of the Gurus, Bhai Vir Singh wrote poetry and fiction. He penned eight collections of poetry: his epic *Rana Surat Singh* (12,000 lines of verse modeled on Edmund Spenser's *The Faerie Queene*) published in 1905 is perhaps the most notable of these, while several anthologies of his shorter poems appeared in the 1920s. This form of the short poem was an innovation in Punjabi literature and became instantly popular. An anthology of songs in praise of the Sikh Gurus was published in 1933 under the title of *Kambdi Kalai* (The trembling wrist). His last collection, *Mere Sainyan Jio*, was published in 1953 and won the prestigious Sahitya Academy Award.

Bhai Vir Singh's novels include *Sundari, Bijay Singh, Satvant Kaur*, and *Baba Naudh Singh*. *Sundari* is the first novel in the Punjabi language, and all of Bhai Vir Singh's fictional works depict strong female protagonists. Sundari, Sushil Kaur, Satvant Kaur, Subhagji, and Rani Raj Kaur serve as paradigms of moral strength, spiritual sensitivity, and physical courage, embodying the Sikh writer's ideals. Widows – shunned in his patriarchal culture – appear as major protagonists.[18]

With Sikh sponsorship, Puran Singh (1881–1931) studied science at the University of Tokyo. Here he absorbed Asian and American philosophical and literary currents and was inspired by the aesthetic philosophy of the Buddhist writer Okakura Kakuzo. Another influence was the free verse and radical optimism of Walt Whitman's *Leaves of Grass*. Attracted also by the

Hindu ascetic Swami Rama Tiratha, Puran Singh gave up his Sikh items of faith and adopted the ocher robe. But on meeting Bhai Vir Singh at a Sikh congress in 1912, he returned to his Sikh way of life. Puran Singh expressed the Sikh Gurus' philosophy in multiple genres in English and Punjabi. He praises Walt Whitman, because like the Sikh Gurus, the American poet transcended divisions and particularities:

> He had glimpses of cosmic consciousness, and in him alone, the human mind, so prone to indulge in analysis and explanation, even in poetry, is plunged again and again into the unknown wholeness of divine feeling.[19]

Puran Singh cites the Gurus profusely, simultaneously interpreting them from a kaleidoscopic perspective of poets Eastern and Western that nurture the human spirit.

The Muslim Firoz Din Sharaf (1898–1955) too extols the Sikh Gurus, Sikh scripture, the creation of the Khalsa by Guru Gobind Singh in 1699, the rule of Maharaja Ranjit Singh, and the heroism of the Sikhs in the independence movement. Unlike other Muslim poets, he dedicated his life to the advancement of the Punjabi language, while bringing in Persian and Arabic vocabulary and metaphors from his Muslim heritage. In his lyrics, Sharaf sketches popular episodes of Guru Nanak's biography imprinted on the collective Sikh memory: the tree stands still to provide shade to the sleeping Guru, the granary he worked in remained perpetually full in spite of him giving away generously to the poor, with his outstretched palm Guru Nanak stops a huge rock hurled at him, his shroud is left without the body and flowers are found instead so both Hindus and Muslims carry them away – to cremate or bury according to their respective customs. Poetically he reproduces the central feature of Guru Nanak's personality: "*Hindu kahin sāḍā, muslim kahin sāḍā*" – "Hindus say he belongs to us; Muslims say he belongs to us."

These writers belong to a linguistic and cultural world shared by the Hindus, Muslims, and Sikhs alike. But as their religious communities increasingly came into conflict during the later years of the British Raj, linguistic parochialism dismembered their common mother tongue.[20]

POSTCOLONIAL WRITING IN INDIA

Since the division of the Punjab between Pakistan and the Republic of India in 1947, and the resultant mass migration and loss of life, many artists, poets, fiction writers, and filmmakers from both sides of the Indo-Pak border have been creating works to expand the emotional reservoir and open up new imaginaries for a shared humanity.

Mohan Singh (1905–1978) was a prolific poet who drew diverse scenarios and effective metaphors to voice his urgent themes of social equality, political unity, and religious pluralism. In 1959 he won the Sahitya Academy Award for one of his collections, *Vaḍḍā Velā*. In his oeuvre the poet returns to the idyllic Punjab where Muslims and Hindus and Sikhs once freely interacted, and wishes for his ashes to be immersed in the Chenab River, now in Pakistan:

> The spirit of Heer and Sohni
> Flow with the Chenab,
> Their feet walk its currents,
> So immerse my ashes in the Chenab!

At a time when the Punjabis were murdering each other in communal frenzy, the Sikh poet ardently remembers the landscape of love immortalized by Punjabi Muslim poets Bullhe Shah and Waris Shah. His poem "Come Let's Dance" seethes with patriotic sentiments. In tune with Guru Nanak's philosophy, Mohan Singh reflects on the mental slavery of his countrymen and women and beckons them to come out of their "curtains and veils" – their hegemonies of caste and class, their segregation of gender and religion, their divisions of *we* and *they*. In Mohan Singh's vibrant verse, rich and poor, black and white, Muslim and Hindu, old and young, men and women join together. His sonorous melodies dance out inclusivity, freedom, and ecstasy.

Amrita Pritam (1919–2005), an Indian feminist poet, novelist, and short-story writer, was the first woman recipient of India's prestigious Sahitya Academy Award and the first woman to receive the Padma Shri; in 1982 she received the Jnanpith Award for her lifetime contributions to Punjabi literature. (She also wrote extensively in Hindi and Urdu.) Her novel *Pinjar* (Skeleton), adapted into film by director Chandra Prakash Dwivedi, was translated by Khushwant Singh, the author of *Train to Pakistan*. In her poetry, fiction, and autobiography, Pritam hauntingly relays the Partition experience.

Pritam's feminist spirit emerges in all her writing, but it is in her poetry that we find its most subtle and boldly sensuous articulation. Her *Ode to Waris Shah* reminds us that the land of the five rivers and the land of the sons (heard in the verse of the male poets) is the land of daughters as well. Pritam speaks for the women who were brutally silenced. In many poems she powerfully protests at the violence against Muslim, Sikh, and Hindu women – victims of abduction, rape, and carnage during the fateful events of 1947. We are also forced to examine the perpetuation of that horrific cruelty to the succeeding generations. Pritam's poem "Helpless" ends with

> Who would know
> How difficult it is
> To bear flagrant violence?
> for a womb to carry life?
> for limbs to burn?
> for bones to char?
> I am a fruit of that time
> when the berries of independence
> were beginning to sprout.
> *My mother's womb was helpless.*

Pritam keeps digging deeper into the layers of sexism. In the poem "Gift of the Virgin" (*Kanyā Dān*) she unmasks the tragic reality behind wedding customs that continue to be vitally important in modern India. The gift (*dān*) *of* and *to* and *for* the virgin daughter (*kanyā*) encompassed by her title "*Kanyā Dān*" is prized in Indian homes. The dowry, as we may recall, was criticized by the fourth Guru (chapter 1), yet giving gifts to the daughter still proves to be an intolerable obligation. Allied with "material" gifts, the daughter is viewed as an economic liability for her family. Skillfully utilizing funerial imagery, Pritam exposes festive marriage scenes as processes of manipulation and exploitation. The bridal henna designs are blotched, the sari the bride wears is more of a shroud, and the expensive jewels only manacle the young virgin:

Blotched in auspicious henna
Shrouded in shimmering crimson,
Bound in chains of yellow gold –
Part of his flesh, daughter of her womb.
O great father, O great mother,
How many blessings you gather!
. . .
A diamond never cries
A cow never speaks
A virgin is ever voiceless.

Pritam's poetry continues to have enormous relevance at every stage of life.[21]

Shiv Kumar Batalvi (1936–1973), though not a Sikh, is celebrated by Sikhs and others as the product of the "literary union of Amrita Pritam and Mohan Singh." At home and in diasporic communities, Punjabis organize "Shiv nights," operas, and symposiums. Batalvi was the youngest recipient of the Sahitya Academy Award, which he won for his epic verse play *Luna* in 1967. His poem "*Dudh dā Qatal*" (Murdering Mother's Milk) is a stunning flashback of the brutal sundering of his motherland. He blames religious communalism for indoctrinating the masses, and charges people from both sides of the Indo-Pak border to take responsibility for the heinous act they executed "together" (*ral ke*). He also reminds people of the Jallianwala Bagh tragedy of 1919 and summons up freedom fighters Udham Singh (1899–1940) and Kartar Singh Sarabha (1896–1915) who died as martyrs.

Other twentieth-century writers include Pritam Singh Safeer, Gurmukh Singh Musafir, Hira Singh Dard, Charan Singh, Jaswant Singh Neki; novelists Ajeet Cour, Dalip Kaur Tiwana, Sant Singh Sekhon, Surinder Singh Narula, Nanak Singh, Narinderpal Singh, Jaswant Singh Kanwal; playwrights I.C. Nanda, Balwant Gargi, Roshan Lal Ahuja, Harcharan Singh, Amrik Singh, Gurdial Singh Phul, Surjit Singh Sethi, Sheila Bhatia,

Ajmer Singh Aulakh; short-story writers Kulwant Singh Virk, Kartar Singh Duggal, and many more. Several of them write in multiple genres.

DIASPORA SIKH WRITING AND FILM

Diaspora Sikhs have also achieved literary distinction, including the Canadian novelist Shauna Singh Baldwin, author of *What the Body Remembers* (1999), a heart-rending narrative arising from the Partition of 1947 which leads readers into the historical reality from the perspective of a Sikh woman. Among the many British Sikh writers, Sunjeev Sahota published *The Year of the Runaways* (2003) and the journalist Sathnam Sanghera authored *The Boy with the Topknot, a Memoir of Love, Secrets and Lies in Wolverhampton* (2008) as well as *Marriage Material* (2013). Nav K. Gill, who wrote *Under the Moonlit Sky* (2010), and Amarjit Sidhu, author of *No Way Home* (2010), are Canadian Sikhs.

Many first-generation Sikh immigrants have composed, recited, and published their poetry, novels, and plays in Punjabi. In the United Kingdom, Punjabi writer, editor, translator, and activist Amarjit Chandan has published extensively. Rupinderpal Singh Dhillon from West London writes novels, short stories, and poetry in a British form of Punjabi which he taught himself. Likewise in Canada, Ajmer Rode has published books of poetry, plays, nonfiction, and translation in Punjabi and English. Also active in the Writers Union of Canada are Nadim Parmar, Sadhu Binning, and poet, dramatist, short story writer, and translator Surjeet Kalsey.

British Sikh playwright Gurpreet Kaur Bhatti's plays include *Behsharam, Behud, Khāndān*, and *Behztī*. In 2004 the Birmingham premiere of *Behztī* was canceled because of Sikh protests at Bhatti's inclusion of a rape supposedly occurring in a gurdwara. The cancellation drew vociferous condemnation of this denial of free speech by distinguished personalities in the arts.

Diaspora Sikh poets include Daljit Nagra in the United Kingdom and Rupi Kaur in Canada. Nagra imitates the English spoken by Indian immigrants who grew up in the Punjab. In 2004 he won the Forward Poetry Prize for best single poem, "Look We Have Coming to Dover!" Nagra voices the racism and mockery experienced by the first wave of uneducated Sikh Punjabi immigrants in England, including his parents. His poem "A Black History of the English-Speaking Peoples" appeared in the *New Yorker* (18th July 2011). Rupi Kaur is a Canadian national activist, artist, and author of the *New York Times* best-selling poetry collections *milk and honey* and *the sun and her flowers*. Her bite-sized free-verse poetry coupled with simple illustrations is characteristic of the new age of Instagram poets (Instapoets). In her minimalist style, Kaur captures the pain and abuse in the lived experience of womanhood:

> when my mother opens her mouth / to have a conversation at dinner / my father shoves the word hush / between her lips and tells her to never speak with her mouth full / this is how the women in my family / learned to live with their mouths closed
>
> *milk and honey* (2015), 35

Rupi understands her own writing to be cathartic, to be a limb, an extension of her being.

In the United States Sikh women are writing their personal accounts to empower themselves and women across cultures. Editor Meeta Kaur has brought together two collections: *Her Name Is Kaur: Sikh American Women Write about Love, Courage, and Faith* (2014) and *Kaurs Reimagine: Sikh Women Blaze New Trails* (2014). Sikh unicity shatters the patrilineal system of naming, so throughout their lives Sikh women retain their common female surname "Kaur" with its authentic subjectivity. Sadly, the collection *Kaurs Reimagine* by 25 multigenerational women and gender queer, nonbinary, and gender-nonconforming individuals exposes their oppressive internalized patriarchy. But the Kaurs also find a way out by turning to the liberating principles of their Gurus. Raw and real, their firsthand accounts of abuse, violence, infertility, cancer, death, otherness, and more make a profound plea that Sikh ideals be lived out in the here and now.

Film director Gurinder Chadha, a British Sikh from an East African background, has pioneeringly created the films *What's Cooking* (2000), *Bend It like Beckham* (2002), *Bride and Prejudice* (2004), *Angus, Thongs and Perfect Snogging* (2008), *It's a*

Wonderful Afterlife (2010), and *Viceroy's House* (2017) which focuses on the events leading to Partition. *Bend It like Beckham*, Chadha's greatest box office hit, sensitively explores ethnic, racial, religious, and gendered identity. "Bending the ball" is actually bending one's conventional roles so that dreams can come true. The images of Guru Nanak and David Beckham are frequently flashed on Chadha's screen, empoweringly juxtaposing the protagonist's Sikh heritage with her Western dream.

PAINTERS

The award-winning Sikh artist Phoolan Rani (born in Amritsar in 1923) has evocatively illustrated biographies of Guru Nanak, Guru Tegh Bahadar, and Guru Gobind Singh. For Guru Nanak's fifth birth centennial in 1969, she wrote the life of the Guru and illustrated it with 40 remarkable paintings. Phoolan Rani's female eyes catch the presence of women in the first Guru's life. Not only does she show us the female relatives of the Guru but also women from his village and town – women who saw Nanak go to school and who attended his various rites of passage. She captures Nanaki gently leading Nanak, her brother, forward into a new world.[22]

Arpita Singh (born in pre-partitioned Bengal in 1937) received the Padma Bhushan Award from the government of India in 2011. She absorbed the local *kantha* embroidery technique with which she weaves designs in vibrant colors to illuminate the textual body, the Guru Granth Sahib. In her illustrations for the *Hymns of Guru Nanak* (translated by Khushwant Singh),[23] Arpita Singh lyrically sets Punjabi folk tradition in Persian miniature layouts. Inscribed in her modernist style reminiscent of the biblical illustrations of Marc Chagall, Arpita evocatively illustrates pluralism, and woman-centered spirituality.[24]

Devinder Singh (b. 1947), internationally known for his realistic and abstract art, paints events deeply etched into the Sikh consciousness. His works, fusing traditional popular art with cubism to recall Sikh historical moments, are displayed in Sikh sacred spaces and in museums across India and abroad. He is the beloved illustrator for the Sikh comics of Amar Chitra Katha, and the recipient of numerous awards and honors. His paintings for the Sikh Foundation Calendar 2012 are particularly significant for depicting the contributions of Sikh women from Bibi Nanaki to Maharani Jindan.

Arpana Caur (b. 1954) is one of India's foremost contemporary painters. Daughter of the feminist author Ajeet Cour, she effectively conveys communal violence, sexism, bigotry, environmental injustice, and poverty, so confronting audiences with a range of Sikh subjects to provoke critical reflection. Titled *1947*, Arpana's painting of her grandfather carrying the Guru Granth Sahib wrapped in green materials on his head, and a bundle of white cloudlike memories on his hunched back, registers the displacement and carnage during the Partition of the Punjab. Similarly, Arpana's *1984* is a traumatic reminder of the massacre at the Golden Temple by the Indian government, and the killings of innocent Sikhs that followed the assassination of Prime Minister Indira Gandhi by her Sikh bodyguards. For Sikh spectators, the severed head in *1984* is also a reminder of Guru Tegh Bahadar's sacrifice for the freedom of religion in 1675 and of the Five Beloved Sikhs who were ready to offer their head to Guru Gobind Singh during his creation of the Khalsa in 1699. Her painting *Sacred Thread* alludes to the *janamsākhī* event of the *upanayāna*, the Hindu initiation ceremony exclusively performed for the upper-caste "twice-born" boys, during which a young Nanak refused to wear the thread spun by the Brahmin priest. On Arpana's canvas, instead of a youngster discoursing with his family priest, a glowing, white-bearded Nanak amid various hues of yellow is spiritedly cutting the thread coming down his right shoulder across his chest and down his waist with a pair of scissors. The many scissors speckled around are dancing, awaiting to be grabbed by human hands so Guru Nanak's liberating deed is reenacted.

Artists are taking up contemporary issues to inspire action for the egalitarian world championed by the Gurus. Social, political, and environmental justice emotively fuse on their canvas. Sukhpreet Singh (b. 1970) visually conveys how, in 2021, at the peak of the COVID-19 pandemic, men and women took up the stigmatized job of performing the last rites for contagious patients, burying or cremating them with dignity according to their respective faiths (Khanuja collection). Singh's depiction of the farmers' protest against the laws imposed by the government in India (2020–2021) (see chapter 7) similarly celebrates Sikh ideals of inclusivity, generosity, courage, and justice in action. His painting teems with diverse men and women engaged in multiple activities while water cannons are fired, slogans are shouted, tractors are driven, food is cooked and served, all while the scene is being filmed (Khanuja collection). Women are vitally present, and the "enemy" police are heartily served *langar*.

Avtar Singh (b. 1982) exposes the effects of environmental pollution. In *Mata Dharat Mahat, Guru Nanak in Modern Fields* (2022), he re-creates a traditional *janamsākhī* scene: the founder Guru is watching plants being sprayed by pesticides and paddy crop stubble being burned! With the Guru, audiences question the devastation of the beautiful Punjabi landscape wrought by human greed. Sikh artists are taking up key economic-sociopolitical-environmental issues that relate to new lived realities around the world.

ART IN DIASPORA

The twin sisters Amrit and Rabindra Kaur Singh have created a genre they call "Past Modern," a skilled reworking of the traditional Indian miniature style and techniques developed in the Mughal imperial court with their own postcolonial diasporic experience. *All That I Am* vividly reproduces the immigrant story of their father.[25] A smiling Sikh man with a yellow turban and a stethoscope around his neck is in the center and the striking intersection between the framed photos of his parents back in the Punjab and the photo of his wife and children highlights his role in passing the culture and religion of his ancestors in the Punjab to his next generation in the United Kingdom.

Another of their paintings (*Nineteen Eighty-Four*) offers a biting critique of Indian troops' storming of the Golden Temple under the orders of Prime Minister Indira Gandhi.[26] The Golden Temple is framed in an angular perspective, and its *sarovar* is full of the blood of innocent devotees while a multiheaded Indira Gandhi stands in an armored tank, holding a bag of coins in her left hand. With her right, she rejects the martyred heads of the ninth Sikh Guru, Tegh Bahadar, and the freedom fighter

Bhagat Singh. The Singh twins also boldly subvert colonial narratives. Thus, their *Casualty of War* contrasts with the subjugated, romanticized Duleep Singh painted by Franz Winterhalter, at Queen Victoria's request, on Duleep Singh's arrival in London. The twins restore the royal seal of the "Lion of the Punjab" in his son's ring – no more Queen Victoria as in his ring painted by Winterhalter. And the Koh-i-Noor, the quintessential symbol of sovereignty and power that Duleep Singh had placed on Queen Victoria's hand during the Winterhalter week, is strikingly visible on his brown body.

In soft colors, Canadian-born artist and architect Keerat Kaur recalls the valor of Guru Gobind Singh's young martyr sons standing calmly as the walls immuring them go higher and higher; their inspirational grandmother, Mata Gujari, is seen on the left of Keerat Kaur's composition. In California, Sarabjit Singh painted Duleep Singh's daughter, the suffragette Sophia Duleep Singh. Since the Partition of the Punjab in 1947, Sikhs from India were unable to access their historical sites in Pakistan, so Saira Wasim (originally from Lahore and now in the United States) brilliantly catches the triumphant joy of a group sitting in a Rolls-Royce going along the Kartarpur corridor in 2019 with a Sikh flag and musical instruments in their hands.

Harleen Kaur from New Jersey creates spiritually focused murals in pen, ink, and acrylic paint that express her passion for her Sikh heritage, justice, and community building. Nisha Kaur Sethi is an activist artist from Berkeley, California. Influenced by political art and movements from the 1960s, she creates hand-painted posters that have been carried by thousands of protesters. The UK-based Kanwal Dhaliwal has portrayed Amrita Pritam amid a sea of corpses against the map of divided Punjab: Pritam's classic Punjabi poem on the Partition of India (*Ajj Akhan Waris Shah Nun*) is written in the Gurmukhi script seen on the Indian side of the line and in Shahmukhi on the Pakistan side. On Kanwal's canvas, the poet and her verse poignantly disclose the pain and harshness of the cartographic rupture. Women's suffering in a patriarchal society and the experience of being Black/South Asian in Britain infuses the multimedia work of Kenya-born Symrath Patti, another UK-based Sikh artist.

Along with an urgent sense of responsibility, there is a new confidence among diasporic Sikhs that empowers them with an identity that is equally American, British, or Canadian as it is Sikh. Artists, poets, novelists, short story writers, fashion designers, filmmakers, and musicians are exploring their Sikh heritage as well as creating affinities with other cultures they encounter in their lives. It is an exciting time.

The intersection of the Sikh past and the present is strikingly projected by the famous Muslim artist MF Hussain (Khanuja collection). Here we see the first Guru offering viewers unicity written out on the small book on his left side, which we read as a prefiguration of the capacious Guru Granth Sahib. In his right hand, Guru Nanak holds a circle of beads, his iconic marker depicted in numerous *janamsākhī* paintings. Is it *tasbih*? *Rosary*? *Threngwa*? *Japa mala*? *Tulsi mala*? *Rudraksa mala*? Does it belong to Hindus? Muslims? Buddhists? Jains? Christians? Jews? In the artistic symbiosis flashed by Hussain, Guru Nanak's rosary reaches out to welcome the infinite One, offering Sikh, Hindu, Muslim, Christian, and Jewish audiences alike a glimpse of the variegated multiverse beaded on the singular strand, *ikkoankār*.

NOTES

1 Wassily Kandinsky, *Concerning the Spiritual in Art* (New York: Dover, 1977), 54.
2 Mohinder Singh, *Shabad Guru: Illustrated Catalogue of Rare Guru Granth Sahib Manuscripts* (New Delhi: Bhai Vir Singh Sahitya Sadan, 2015).
3 Jeevan Deol, "Illustration and Illumination in Sikh Scriptural Manuscripts," in *New Insights into Sikh Art*, ed. Kavita Singh (Mumbai: The Marg Foundation, 2003), 50–67.
4 See B.N. Goswamy and Caron Smith, *I See No Stranger: Early Sikh Art and Devotion* (New York: Rubin Museum of Art, 2006), 38.
5 W.H. McLeod, *Popular Sikh Art* (Delhi: Oxford University Press, 1991), 5–6. More manuscripts are now coming to light.
6 For details, see Nikky-Guninder Kaur Singh, "Guru Nanak at the Asian Art Museum; a Biography in the Language of Colors," in *Sikh Art from the Kapany Collection*, ed. Paul Michael Taylor and Sonia Dhami (Palo Alto: The Sikh Foundation, in association with the Asian Cultural History Program, Smithsonian Institution, 2017), 99–116.
7 W.H. McLeod, ed. and trans., *Chaupa Singh Rahit-Nama* (Otago: University of Otago Press, 1987), 556, 567.

8 For details, see Nikky-Guninder Kaur Singh, *The Birth of the Khalsa: A Feminist Re-memory of Sikh Identity* (Albany: State University of New York Press, 2005).
9 These couplets are cited by, for example, Parvinder Khanuja, *Splendors of Punjab Heritage* (New Delhi: Roli, 2022), 355 and A.S. Melikian-Chirvani, "Ranjit Singh and the Image of the Past," in *The Arts of the Sikh Kingdoms*, ed. Susan Stronge (London: V&A Publications, 2001), 63. See also Jyoti M. Rai, "The Nanakshahi – The Divine Sikh Coinage," in *Sikh Art from the Kapany Collection*, ed. Paul Michael Taylor and Sonia Dhami (Palo Alto: The Sikh Foundation, 2017), 219–235.
10 Edwin Lord Weeks, *From the Black Sea through Persia and India* (New York: Harper, 1896), 186.
11 All these paintings by British women are reproduced in Eleanor Nesbitt, *Sikh: Two Centuries of Western Women's Art and Writing* (London: Kashi House, 2024).
12 F.S. Aijazuddin, *Sikh Portraits by European Artists* (London: Sotheby Parke Bernet, Karachi and Delhi, Oxford University Press, 1979), 30.
13 Aijazuddin, *Sikh Portraits*, illustration II (reproduced by Amrit Kaur Singh and Rabindra Kaur Singh, *Twin Perspectives: Paintings by Amrit and Rabindra KD Kaur Singh* (Liverpool:Twin Studio, plate 40).
14 Aijazuddin, *Sikh Portraits by European Artists*, illustration III.
15 The Dexter Collection Part II (16th July 2021 12:00 Chiswick auction).
16 Vivan Sundaram, ed., *Amrita Sher-Gil: A Self-Portrait in Letters and Writings* (New Delhi: Tulika Books, 2010), 1:325.
17 For details, see Nikky-Guninder Kaur Singh, "Panj Pyarian: Artistic Expressions of Sikh Existentiality," in *Global Sikhs*, ed. D. Jakobsh and O. Takhar (Abingdon: Routledge, 2023), 215–238.
18 Nikky-Guninder Kaur Singh, *Feminine Principle in the Sikh Vision of the Transcendent* (Cambridge: Cambridge University Press, 1993), 150–241, analyzes Bhai Vir Singh's women protagonists.
19 Puran Singh, *The Spirit of Oriental Poetry* (London: Kegan Paul, Trench, Trubner & Co., Ltd., 1926), 28.
20 Translations from the original by Nikky-Guninder Kaur Singh, *Of Sacred and Secular Desire: An Anthology of Lyrical Writings from the Punjab* (London: I.B. Tauris, 2012), 174–190.
21 Nikky-Guninder Kaur Singh, *Of Sacred and Secular Desire*, 191–232, is devoted to Amrita Pritam's works.
22 Painting by Phulan Rani, in *Life of Guru Nanak through Pictures* (Amritsar: Modern Sahit Academy, 1969), 17.
23 Khushwant Singh, trans., *Hymns of Guru Nanak* (Hyderabad: Orient Longman, 1991).
24 Nikky-Guninder Kaur Singh, "Panj Pyarian," 215–238.
25 Amrit Kaur Singh and Rabindra Kaur Singh, *Twin Perspectives*, 81.
26 Amrit Kaur Singh and Rabindra Kaur Singh, *Twin Perspectives*, 67.

REFERENCES AND FURTHER READING

Brown, Kerry. *Sikh Art and Literature*. London: Routledge, 1999.

Nesbitt, Eleanor. *Sikh: Two Centuries of Western Women's Art and Writing*. London: Kashi House, 2024.

Singh, Nikky-Guninder Kaur. *Janamsakhi: Paintings of Guru Nanak in Early Sikh Art*. New Delhi: Roli, 2023.

Singh, Nikky-Guninder Kaur. *Of Sacred and Secular Desire: An Anthology of Lyrical Writings from the Punjab*. London: I.B. Tauris, 2012.

Stronge, Susan, ed. *The Arts of the Sikh Kingdom*. London: V&A Publications, 1999.

Taylor, Paul Michael, and Sonia Dhami. *Sikh Art from the Kapany Collection*. Palo Alto: The Sikh Foundation, in association with the Asian Cultural History Program, Smithsonian Institution, 2017.

7

CONTEMPORARY CHALLENGES AND FUTURE PROSPECTS

The vitality of the Sikh community in the 21st century is unmistakable, whether in the construction of gurdwaras, the growth of Sikh studies, notably in North American universities, or in the prominence of Sikhs in public life in the United Kingdom, Canada, and the United States as well as in India. Chapter 6 has offered a glimpse of Sikhs' wonderful and ever-expanding contributions to the arts – to visual art, film, literature, and drama – and how so much of this creative output is fed by their distinctive Sikh spiritual heritage as well as by traumatic historical events.

HISTORICAL PROGNOSES

Yet, as early as the 19th century, some prognoses for the survival of Sikhism were pessimistic, and some authoritative 20th-century accounts, too, cast doubt on Sikhs continuing at all as a distinct community and suggested that their religion was moribund. For instance, in 1895, a book by Anne Campbell Wilson, a British travel writer and musicologist, whose husband was financial commissioner of Punjab, declared, "In the Punjaub [*sic*], Buddhism and Sikhism alike have dwindled into mere Hindu sects."[1] Then, publishing in 1909, Max Arthur Macauliffe, the much-respected Irish authority on – and champion of – the Sikh religion, stated categorically that "Hinduism has embraced Sikhism in its folds; the still comparatively young religion is making a vigorous struggle for life, but its ultimate destruction is, it is apprehended, inevitable without State support."[2]

DOI: 10.4324/9781003359210-7

Macauliffe had, moreover, pointed out that there was "hardly any one Sikh" who could translate the "sacred writings" correctly.[3]

In a similar vein, publishing 90 years after Macauliffe, the distinguished journalist and noted writer on Sikhs' history Khushwant Singh concluded pessimistically, "At times it appears that perhaps the Khalsa have run the course of history prescribed for them and that their Gurus in their inscrutable wisdom have given them leaders who will fulfil their death-wish."[4] Khushwant Singh portrayed a religious life that had "declined into meaningless ritual" while "discrimination against lower-caste Sikhs" still persisted. He lamented the continuing outbreaks of anti-Hindu violence perpetrated by some Sikhs in Punjab.[5]

In other words, in the early 20th century, the two main threats to the wider recognition of the Sikh religion and, indeed, to its very survival were, according to Macauliffe's diagnosis, on the one hand, the lack of people who could fully understand – let alone translate into English – the complex linguistic interweaving of the language(s) of the Guru Granth Sahib and, on the other hand, Hinduism's proven tendency to swallow up smaller Indic faith traditions. What was more, by the end of the century (in Khushwant Singh's view, at least) Sikhs' behavior fell far short of the religion's principles of creating a casteless society with a respect for all human life.

Nonetheless, despite these negative prognostications, now as it enters the second quarter of the 21st century, Sikhism is the fifth largest "world religion," Sikhs live in many parts of the world, gurdwaras are thriving, and other Sikh institutions are proliferating. Sikhs' commitment to community service has become increasingly far reaching and high profile, and more and more Sikhs are achieving prominence in their professional lives.

FARMERS' PROTEST, 2020–2021

Notably, too, Sikhs' confidence as a community was strengthened by their role in the world's largest ever farmers' protest, from November 2020 to November 2021. The Punjab farmers' protests demonstrated how concerted courageous action can still be energized by the Sikh community's remembered history of previous centuries' resilient resistance to rulers' oppression.[6]

The protesters, most of them Sikh farmers from Punjab, opposed three laws that the Indian government had passed the previous September. These would have deregulated agriculture in ways that, farmers feared, would be ruinous to their livelihoods. At considerable cost to their families, tens of thousands of farmers camped for a year on the outskirts of Delhi until, in November 2021, the government repealed the laws. The protesting farmers endured sustained hardship and some lost their lives. Their resolve was galvanized by the community's memory of confrontation over several centuries with oppressive Delhi-based overlords. Symbolically, on India's Republic Day, 21st January, a Sikh farmer hoisted the *nishān sāhib* (Sikh pennant), albeit briefly, on Delhi's Red Fort. Sikhs' tradition of *sevā* too meant that, as mentioned in chapter 4, they were fed by daily *langar*s (and given blankets) and the protest itself is now, with its songs, slogans, and strength of purpose, a part of Sikhs' heritage of proud memories.

The backdrop to such episodes of resurgent struggle and optimism continues to be challenges both from within the Sikh community and from outside.

RELIGIOUS REALIGNMENT AND DEMOGRAPHY

In the 1966 edition of his history of the Sikhs, Khushwant Singh had stated firmly that "the only chance of survival of the Sikhs as a separate community is to create a state in which they form a compact group, where the teaching of Gurmukhi and the Sikh religion is compulsory, and where there is an atmosphere of respect for their Khalsa forefathers."[7] As we saw in chapter 2, that very same year the boundaries of India's Punjab state were indeed redrawn with the result that Sikhs did become a substantial majority (being 60.2 percent, according to the 1971 census) in the new, smaller Punjab. However, by 2011 that had fallen to 57 percent, as more Sikhs had migrated overseas and Hindu and Muslim laborers had moved in from other North Indian states. The percentage decline looks set to continue. In fact, Sikhs may already no longer constitute the majority even in Indian Punjab.

CHRISTIANITY

Another reason for declining numbers is that in the 2020s, the number of Sikhs who are converting to Christianity, especially in Punjab, is increasing. Indeed, in its anxiety about this trend, the SGPC launched a new movement, Ghar Ghar Andar Dharamsāl – its name, meaning "Within every home let there be a sacred shrine," is from a poem by the revered 15th- to 16th-century Sikh Bhai Gurdas. The movement's teams of Sikh preachers fight the perceived menace of conversion. Meanwhile, sporadic attacks by Sikhs on pastors and churches and clashes between local Sikhs and missionaries are increasing. In 2022, the leader of the Sikhs' Amritsar-based body, the Akāl Takht, alleged coercive conversion by Christian missionaries and demanded an anti-conversion law (as in other states).

At the same time, when population figures are updated, they may well not reveal the full extent of the continuing shift toward Christian congregations. This is because the appeal of Christianity is mainly to the Dalits, who constitute 32 percent of Punjab's population, and if they were to identify themselves officially as Christian, they would forfeit their caste reservation benefits. Thus, many Punjabis may believe in Christ, while maintaining their official Sikh identity and their traditional Sikh life cycle rites.

Since the 1970s, in addition to Punjab's longer-standing Catholic and Church of North India churches, Pentecostal and Evangelical groups from both outside and within Punjab have given fresh dynamism to Protestant Christians. Evangelists use words that are evocative for Sikhs (such as *sangat* for "congregation," *Waheguru* for "God," and *Satguru* for "Jesus") and use devotional songs – adapted to a Christian message – that are already familiar from Sikh tradition. In such ways they make their teaching more easily acceptable to would-be converts. However, the drift from Sikh to Christian allegiance stems not only from the concerted efforts of Christian evangelists but from the discrimination that Dalit Sikhs encounter at the hands of higher-caste Sikhs despite the Gurus' clear teaching to the contrary. For example, Dalit Sikhs' experience is of being unwelcome in gurdwaras managed by Jat Sikhs: Jat Sikhs' humiliation of Dalits has made them susceptible to conversion. By contrast, the church brings them a sense of belonging and other benefits including miraculous faith healing (not always genuine in its detractors' eyes) and protection from evil spirits, plus the hope at least of free education to postgraduate level, employment, free hospital treatment, and reportedly, assurances about UK and Canadian visas for converts' children.

Not only the religious demography of Punjab but also the state's political landscape look set to change, as parties that allow Christian evangelizing can win the bloc votes of the Christian minority. In April 2023, at the Pentecostal Open Door Church in Kapurthala, Christian organizations and leaders in Punjab launched the first Christian-affiliated political party, the United Punjab Party (UPP). The launch took place under the auspices of the Pentecostal Christian Parbandhak Committee (modeled on the SGPC), whose aim is to represent the local Christian community's interests, such as their demand for Christian graveyards in Punjab.

DERĀS

As explained by Professor Dharam Singh,[8] a Punjab-based Sikh scholar, since the 1990s a single family has controlled the Akali Dal political party which has, in turn, controlled the SGPC. With the weakening of the SGPC, *derā*s (sectarian centers that are focused on a particular powerful personality) and caste-based gurdwaras have proliferated at the same time as the upsurge in Christian conversions of Sikhs from "lower" castes.

The electoral power of the leaders of *derā*s is certainly a growing element in Punjab's political mix. These individuals can guarantee huge swaths of votes for their favored party. Some observers regard the *derā*s and their leaders as a threat to Sikhism. Like the Christian churches, *derā*s attract many thousands of adherents who feel unwelcome in the predominantly Jat environment of many gurdwaras. Foremost among these *derā*s in Punjab are Derā Sacha Sauda, Radha Soami Satsang Beas, and Derā Sach Khand Ballan. Gurmeet Ram Rahim Singh, one of the leaders of Derā Sacha Sauda, was convicted of serious crimes, and his followers are sometimes assumed to be behind the instances of vandalism of copies of the Guru Granth Sahib (see below). Meanwhile, Derā Sach Khand Ballan in District Jalandhar is the Ravidassia center that manages Ravidassias' preeminent pilgrimage center, the temple at Seer Goverdhanpur (Sir Gobardhan) in Varanasi in the state of Uttar Pradesh.

In 2010, in the Ravidassia temple in Varanasi, Ravidassia was declared to be a separate religion, with Guru Ravi Das as its sole spiritual master. Henceforth, the Amrit Bani Guru Ravidas was to replace the Guru Granth Sahib as the new religion's scripture. It was released by Sant Niranjan Dass, the head of Derā Sach Khand Ballan. From now on, the Ravidassia temple in Varanasi would be the highest seat of temporal authority, the Ravidassias' logo would be the name "Hari" (Lord) in Gurmukhi script and Ravidassias would greet each other with the words "Jai Gurudev" (Guru).

This was not a sudden decision, but the formal split from the Sikh community was triggered by the attack in 2009 in which Sant Niranjan Dass's colleague Swami Rama Nand had been killed in Vienna's Ravidassia gurdwara. The reason was what other Sikhs perceived to be disrespect toward the Guru Granth Sahib as the two Ravidassia leaders from Derā Sachkhand Ballan were being honored on a par with the Guru Granth Sahib.

The main factor, however (at least in Ravidassias' understanding of the lethal aggression), was some other Sikhs' antagonism toward them based on their low-caste status as *chamars* (the hereditary community associated with generations of employment as skinners and tanners). Notably, the Gurus' commitment to embedding and expanding an inclusive community of Guru-oriented devotees has not yet dismantled caste prejudice that undergirds and suffuses Punjabi society. As the sociologist Surinder Jodhka has shown, the opportunities for lower-caste Punjabis continue to be limited by their poorer social capital compared with those from higher-caste backgrounds.

SANTS

More generally, while Sikhs' allegiance to an abundance of ***jathebandīs*** – that is, organizations – which tend to center on a spiritual leader (*sant*) can be regarded as a source of strength and vitality for their adherents, it also undermines Sikh unity. In addition to historical minority groupings such as the Nihangs, the Namdharis, and the Nirmalas, many other Sikhs are today influenced by the spiritual leaders of Damdami Taksal and Nanaksar[9] as well as by other *sant*s. Chapter 5 introduced, for example, the Guru Nanak Nishkam Sewak Jatha, a *sant* succession that holds a strong position in the United Kingdom.

In the 21st century, allegiance to *sant*s looks set to affect key aspects of many Sikhs' lives. For example, it is the influence of a *sant* that leads many Sikhs to take that life-changing step of being initiated into the Khalsa by receiving *amrit*. Their commitment to Khalsa discipline is not only mapped on their bodies – through their adoption of the Five Ks, wearing a turban (which is increasingly the case for women, especially in the diaspora, as well as for men) – but is evident too in their teetotalism and adherence to a strictly lactovegetarian diet. Although it is only the meat of animals that have been slaughtered in accordance with Muslim (or Jewish) procedure that is forbidden according to Sikh *rahit*, the *sant*s and their followers generally understand this prohibition to mean abstention from all meat and meat products.[10]

*Sant*s also motivate their followers' commitment to *sevā*. To take one example in Punjab, Sant Balbir Singh Seechewal champions environmental issues. It was the *kār sevā* (voluntary service through physical labor) of his 3,000 volunteers that in 2000–2003 restored the flow of the clogged Kali Bein River, the river in which, as a young man, Guru Nanak had his transformational experience of *ikkoankār*. Sadly, despite this monumental effort, environmental threats to this river continue.

On occasion, too, when faced by a common challenge, the *sant*s unite as the Sant Samaj (i.e., *sant* association). One such challenge was the attempt to reform the Sikh calendar.

CALENDAR CONTROVERSY

Over the first two and a half decades of the 21st century, the continuing differences of opinion over the Sikh calendar have illustrated tensions between, variously, the SGPC, the Akāl Takht, the Sant Samaj, the Punjab government, the Pakistan

Shiromani Gurdwara Parbandhak Committee, and gurdwara management committees around the world. The motivation to implement a calendar based on different principles from the Vikrami calendar of North India's Hindus, which Sikhs had hitherto shared, demonstrates continuing Sikh concern to distance their religion from Hinduism and to put Sikhism on a par with other world religions. Sikhs who backed calendar reform also saw the advantages of having festival dates that would remain constant, year on year, in relation to the internationally accepted Gregorian calendar.

As long ago as the 1960s a Canadian Sikh, Pal Singh Purewal, had begun researching with a view to giving Sikhs a solar (rather than luni-solar) "Nanakshahi" calendar that would be based in Sikhs' religious tradition and in which dates would not be determined (as they are in the Vikrami calendar) by the moon's phases. In 1998 the SGPC passed a resolution to implement Purewal's reformed calendar, and in December that year the Punjab government announced that Guru Gobind Singh's birthday would accordingly be celebrated on the Nanakshahi date of 5th January 1999. (One of the problems of the older calendar was that in the same year, this particular *gurpurb* could occur both in early January and in late December.) Purewal's calendar is now known as the "Mool [i.e., original, *mūl*] Nanakshahi calendar" as, following objections from the Sant Samaj, in 2003 the SGPC endorsed modifications to it: from now on, Guru Nanak's Birthday, Hola Mohalla, and Bandi Chhoṛ Divas would be consistent with the Vikrami calendar. Accordingly, Guru Nanak's Birthday would be celebrated (as, indeed, it had continued to be in practice) in November on the full moon of Kattak (rather than on 14th April, which would have been in line with the dating given in the more reliable *janamsākhīs*) and Bandi Chhoṛ Divas would be reinstated on the same day as Divālī. In 2010 the SGPC further adapted the calendar so that the dates of some other *gurpurabs* (including Guru Gobind Singh's Birthday and the day marking the martyrdom of Guru Arjan) reverted to the Vikrami dates. Then, in 2014, the SGPC restored a totally Vikrami calendar (e.g., the starting date of the months was once again lunar) although they still called it "Nanakshahi." Since then, a conference in Chicago has adopted the unaltered 1999 Nanakshahi calendar, and in 2020 the Pakistan Shiromani Gurdwara Parbandhak Committee too released the "Mool Nanakshahi calendar." Meanwhile, in practice, the majority of Sikhs worldwide have likely been largely unaware of the controversy.

CURRENT TRENDS AND DILEMMAS

GENDER DISPARITY

As honor-fixated misogyny and routine sexism persist in Punjabi society, one issue with potentially far-reaching consequences for the future of Sikhs and other Punjabis in India and beyond has been the practice of female feticide – in other words, the termination of the lives of unborn girls. Although such sex selection is illegal in India as well as in other countries, the technological advances make it possible to determine the sex of unborn children, and as a result, female fetuses can then be aborted. (Previously, there had been a high incidence of female infanticide – with unwanted babies being stifled at birth by the midwife.) The good news, at the time of writing, is that the ratio of female to male births in Punjab, is increasing – from 892 girls to 1,000 boys in 2014–2015 to 928:1,000 in 2021–2022, and that ratio is growing most markedly in the case of Sikh families.

Efforts are also underway to celebrate the births of girls as well as of boys and to celebrate their academic and sporting achievements. The birth of a boy is traditionally marked by the family distributing special spherical sweetmeats, *ladū*, and now the Pink Ladoo Project in the United Kingdom and Canada encourages the parents of newborn girls to celebrate with pink *ladu*s rather than the usual golden-colored ones.

Could traditional practice at the heart of the wedding ceremony too be changed one day?

Commonly, the bride's father hands each end of a scarf to the couple; instead, both parents could perform this rite, together holding the scarf as they walk over to the couple. Such a gesture would demonstrate that the bride is jointly their daughter, not a possession passing from the father to the husband – that is, from one man to another. The sequence of the gesture could also be changed. Instead of first handing an end of the scarf to the groom and then to the bride (as is the common practice now), parents could start with their daughter, so symbolically erasing the centuries-old image of women as mere followers. It would be a symbolic step toward deconstructing a daughter's dependence on her father before marriage, her husband after marriage, and her son after widowhood. In keeping with the spirit of the Gurus, it would also be more egalitarian for the groom and the bride to take turns in leading the *lāvān*. Currently, the groom leads the four circles around the sacred book. In fact, to take turns would be to fulfill the intrinsic circularity of *lāvān*, which is without beginning or end and thus transcends linear hierarchies.[11]

Some of the Indian celebrations in which Sikhs participate, as mentioned in chapter 4, are clearly gender biased. Thus, Lohṛī is chiefly celebrated in homes where a boy is born. While parents and grandparents of a boy distribute money and gifts around crackling bonfires, a girl's family may feel sad. Likewise, the pan-Indian rite of Rakhṛi celebrates brothers: sisters without brothers or mothers without sons may experience sadness and even abuse. Some specifically Sikh ceremonies too favor boys. Affluent Sikh families now ostentatiously celebrate their sons' *dastār bandhan* (first turban tying). Theoretically, Sikh rites are the same for both girls and boys, but there are double standards.[12] The elaborate name-giving ceremonies of the sons are never quite the same for the daughters! Marriage requires a much larger financial investment from the daughter's family than from her husband's.

Underlying the discrimination against girls is, on the one hand, the prejudice associating girls with the pressure on their parents to pay the ever-increasing cost of marriages, including dowry, even if the word "dowry" is avoided, and additionally, the expectation that in old age, it will be their sons who support them whereas their daughters will be lost to their in-laws' family. It needs to be reiterated that whereas the culture of Punjab reinforces macho and sometimes misogynistic attitudes, the Sikhs' religious teaching points, by contrast, to equality.

Indeed, the Guru Granth Sahib affirms women's creative and natural processes in the social fabric. Not only are there images celebrating gestation, birthing, and lactation but also a condemnation of taboos surrounding menstruation and postpartum pollution.[13] Furthermore, as we have seen, the Gurus' verses suggest their criticism of the *purdah* (confinement of women) and *sati* (self-immolation of women on the funeral pyre of their husband). Their poetry discloses their intention for society to discard oppressive androcentric codes.

Sikh scripture continuously erases negative connotations of women's bodies: pollution is instead the sight that covets "another's wife, wealth, and beauty" (GGS: 472). Guru Nanak reprimanded those who stigmatize the garment stained with menstrual blood as polluted (GGS: 140), and scriptural verses celebrate the female body and affirm the centrality of menstrual blood in the creative process: "From mother's blood and father's semen is created form of infinite beauty" (GGS: 1022). Here priority is given to *ma ki raktu* (mother's blood). Another scriptural passage confirms it – "From blood and semen we are created" (GGS: 706) – and the Sikh Gurus condemned notions of the pollution that was associated with childbirth:

> All pollution is mere doubt,
> Attachment to duality ...
> Nanak, the Guru-centered see through.
> Nothing is polluted for them.
>
> (GGS: 472)

However, because of their menstrual periods, women are still, 500 years later, barred from some types of religious service: they are tacitly forbidden to perform *prakāsh* (daily installing of the Guru Granth Sahib) or *sukhāsan* (nightly ceremonial closing of the Gur Granth Sahib), and women are not permitted to perform *kīrtan* in the Golden Temple. In *Sikhism Today*, Sikh academic Jagbir Jhutti-Johal gives a snapshot of women's exclusion from religious service at the central place of Sikh worship, the Golden Temple:

> Here Sikh women are not allowed to read from the Guru Granth Sahib, play *kirtan* or perform any *sewa* in the sanctum sanctorum (main prayer room). These *sewas* are "reserved" for men only.[14]

Jhutti-Johal also cites the widely publicized discriminatory case from 2003, when two Sikh women were not allowed to even touch the palanquin carrying the Guru Granth Sahib during its evening ritual. Likewise, Opinderjit Takhar, in her case study at a gurdwara in the United Kingdom, describes taboos preventing women from cooking meals and preparing *kaṛāh prashād* during their menstrual period.[15] Many Sikh women will continue to see themselves as polluted and will perpetuate these fallacies through their own daughters and granddaughters unless Sikh men and women consciously shake off body-disparaging, son-privileging codes prescribed in ancient texts and internalized by their North Indian patriarchal society from centuries ago.[16] This is an area in which *sant*s are conspicuously silent, yet their influence could bring about change at least among their own followers.

SEXUALITY

While the thrust of the Gurus' teaching is toward full equality, sexuality is not so clearly referenced as female gender is. The Guru Granth Sahib makes no mention of homosexuality or bisexuality. However, the colorful depiction of Guru Nanak from the 1733 *B-40 Janamsākhī* comfortably conversing with Muslim saint Sheikh Sharaf dressed as a woman in a red sari with heavy jewels is popular with LGBTQI+ Sikhs. It serves as their visual evidence that the progressive Guru Nanak did not condemn cross-dressing or same-sex relationships (www.sarbat.net/).[17] In 2023, after his marriage video had been leaked online, a UK-based Sikh, Jasvir Singh, came out as being not only a devout Sikh but also gay. Thanks to speaking on BBC Radio 4's *Thought for the Day*, he was well known in the United Kingdom as a Sikh voice as well as being a barrister and the founder of City Sikhs and cofounder of the annual South Asian Heritage Month. To quote Jasvir Singh:

> I know that speaking about this is going to be highly controversial. I'm sure there will be lots of people out there who will be upset, annoyed, even angry at me. But I've got nothing to hide and I know that I have got Waheguru [God] with me, as I have had Waheguru with me all the way.[18]

While more Sikhs are coming out and demanding to be accorded the equal treatment which they see as being intrinsic to their religion, Sikh society continues to be generally disapproving of homosexuality. The statement in the Sikh Rahit Maryādā that marriage is between a male and a female means that gay Sikhs are currently barred from having an *anand kāraj* marriage rite. Moreover, an edict in January 2005 from Giani Joginder Singh Vedanti, the Jathedar (custodian) of Sri Akāl Takht Sahib, denounced same-sex marriages and exhorted Sikhs globally to ban such marriages in all gurdwaras. He told visiting Sikh Canadian MPs that their duty was to oppose same-sex marriage. For gay Sikhs, any future developments remain uncertain.

Meanwhile, the internet offers the possibility of online discussion of sexuality, and younger generations appear to be more accepting than their older relatives.

BEADABI

The attack in the Ravidassia gurdwara in Vienna in 2009 had been provoked by allegations of *beadabī* (disrespect) as devotees were perceived by their assailants to be showing honor to the *sant* on a par with the Guru Granth Sahib – or at least this was one factor. Headlines have been made by a spate of incidents of *beadabī*. Literally meaning "disrespect," this term is applied to any behavior that is deemed by detractors to be disrespectful to the Guru Granth Sahib and, more generally, to the Gurus and the *maryādā* (Sikh discipline).

Beadabī is a recurrent issue both in Punjab and in the diaspora, as we saw in chapter 5 with regard to the prohibition of non-Sikhs marrying in the gurdwara. Sikh marriages in Punjab are now, reportedly, solemnized only in the gurdwara because transferring the Guru Granth Sahib temporarily to other wedding venues risks disrespect to the Guru (if, for instance, it is transported inappropriately or if the venue is one where alcohol might be served). Owing to an increase of weddings being conducted in romantic overseas locations, such as beaches in Greece, in October 2023 the Akāl Takht issued a *hukamnāmā* forbidding what are known as "destination weddings."

Disturbingly, since 2014 and persisting into the 2020s, there has also been a series of unsolved incidents of deliberate desecration, often involving the ripping of pages from a gurdwara's Guru Granth Sahib. In the first of these incidents, 110 pages were found lying outside a gurdwara. This is especially distressing as Sikhs cherish each page as an *ang* (literally "a limb") of their embodied Guru, so such vandalism is keenly felt as a willful assault on and dismembering of the Guru.

SUBSTANCE ABUSE

The media also frequently report the high level of drug and alcohol abuse in Punjab and especially among its Sikh population. Despite the fact that both the teaching of the Guru Granth Sahib and the rules in successive codes of conduct unambiguously prohibit using intoxicants and stimulants, Punjabi culture's encouragement of a macho masculinity also encourages the uninhibited consumption of liquor by men. Indeed, popular *bhangṛā* songs reinforce this association. The fact that Punjab's Jat Sikh farmers now employ laborers from other states such as Bihar means that the younger generation of the farmers' families have the time and the means to take recreational drugs as well as to consume alcohol to excess. It remains to be seen whether, and with what social consequences, this trend continues and whether the present gap between men's and women's behavior in this regard continues to lessen.

CALLS FOR AN INDEPENDENT SIKH STATE

In June 2024, in the Indian parliamentary election, Amritpal Singh, a radical pro-Khalistan separatist, was elected as MP in the Lok Sabha despite his currently being a prisoner in jail in Assam. Before his arrest, supporters in the United Kingdom and North America had taken part in angry demonstrations. Indeed, demands for an independent state called Khalistan (an idea first suggested in the 1940s in the run-up to India's independence) continue to be raised by Sikhs in Canada and some other countries. Supporters propagate a narrative – with an undeniable appeal to younger generations of diaspora Sikhs – of Sikhs as victims of the Indian government and they clamor for independence. However, the majority of Sikhs, whether in India or outside, do not support outright separatism or the creation of an independent state, Khalistan, although Sikhs worldwide were understandably alienated from the Indian state by the brutal events of 1984. For most Sikhs in India, any repetition of the trauma of the partition of 1947 is unthinkable and many of those who are sympathetic to the cause are aware of the practical obstacles, not least Sikhs' lack of political unity and the unresolved question of where exactly Khalistan would be established. At the same time, Sikhs worldwide recognize the increasing threat to religious minorities in India that is posed by right-wing Hindu nationalism. As further aggravation to Sikhs, in the 2020s, the government of India tried to discredit the Indian farmers' legitimate demands by disparagingly branding the farmers' movement as Khalistani.[19]

REVIVAL OF TRADITION

Meanwhile, Sikhs' memories and interpretations of earlier periods of history continue to revitalize their tradition, or at least to motivate and inspire enthusiastic minorities within the wider Sikh community, whether this is in learning Sikh martial arts or in learning to play pre-19th-century musical instruments for *kīrtan*.

MARTIAL ART

In the United Kingdom – and subsequently in Italy and India – *shastar vidyā* (literally the "art or science of weaponry") has become popular, principally among young male Sikhs, largely thanks to the initiative of Nidar Singh Nihang. Expertise in wielding traditional weapons revives the Akali-Nihangs' tradition, which had all but disappeared during British rule in India. After 11 years of training in India, Nidar Singh has equipped many more Sikhs with often breathtaking skills in swordsmanship and the use of other weapons which they demonstrate at Sikh festivals. The men's *dumallā*s (particularly tall turbans) emulate the Akali-Nihangs' turbans of previous centuries. In a less high-risk version of *shastar vidyā* known as *gatkā*, combatants demonstrate their dexterity using sticks rather than swords.

WOMEN'S DRESS

For decades members of the Akhand Kirtani Jatha (chapter 2) have interpreted one of the Five Ks as not only prohibiting the shortening or removal of hair but also as requiring them to cover their heads with a *keskī*, a small turban. In Healthy, Happy, Holy Organization (3HO)/Sikh Dharma of the Western Hemisphere, too (chapter 5), women wear turbans – in their case, all-white ones similar to their male counterparts'.

Drawing their inspiration from Sikhs of centuries past – or at least from recent, retrospective depiction of them, especially online – increasing numbers of women, and especially *amritdhārī* women, wear the turban as well as, or in lieu of, the *chunnī* (scarf). Clearly, adoption of the turban signifies commitment to equality between the sexes and an unequivocal allegiance to the Sikh religion.

MUSIC

Kīrtan's instrumental expression ranges from Bhai Mardana's rabāb to the typical 20th-century duo of *tablā* and harmonium. Moreover, sacred music is now being revitalized both by experimentation with Western instruments and by reference to pre-19th-century practice. *Kīrtan* ensembles may nowadays include any of the following instruments: the *sarandā, taus, dilrubā, tānpurā, joṛī/pakhāwaj, santur*, sitar, zithers, violin, cello, mandolin, piano, and even the Australian didgeridoo. Today the more ancient instruments are being revived while various fusions are also underway. There is a call for a return to playing traditional Sikh instruments broadly categorized as *tanti sāz* (string instruments). The "foreign" "colonial" harmonium brought into India by Christian missionaries (see chapter 2) is under attack.[20] Importantly, the United Kingdom has just launched the first "globally recognized" examination in Sikh sacred music as a step toward diversifying music education and acknowledging formally the students' dedication and achievement.[21]

Professional groups from India travel worldwide to perform *kīrtan*, and Sikhs in America, Australia, Africa, and Europe are enthusiastically training in *kīrtan*. Sardar Dya Singh, who created a core musical ensemble of leading musicians in Australia, describes his group's music as "bringing Sikh music to the world and world music to the Sikhs." Ancient instruments are being revived and the typical harmonium-tablā pair is expanding. Little Sikh children can be heard reciting hymns in gurdwaras be it New York City, Reggio Emilia, Dublin, or Dundee. Young American Sikhs have formed Chardi Kala Jatha, which is adding another layer of spiritual intensity to Sikh music. These young Americans, inspired by the Sikh Dharma of the Western Hemisphere/3HO, are steeped in Sikh life and have been training in classical music. A new initiative by Sikh women called Gaavani celebrates the female voice.

Non-Sikhs are becoming a part of *kīrtan* ensembles as well, and although the musicians and instrumentalists may belong to different regions and religions, they are in tune with the basic Sikh precepts. *Kīrtan* has taken place not only in gurdwaras but also in concert halls, museums, classrooms, and even in the White House. It is relayed on the radio, TV, YouTube, Spotify, SoundCloud, iTunes, and other music listening platforms. Incorporating a variety of musical genres, Sikh *kīrtan* today is world music. Sat Kartar Khalsa synthesizes Eastern and Western melodies and opens up Sikh music to a wide Western audience. Pioneer in fusion *kīrtan* music, Shivpreet Singh blends Indian classical music and US pop, folk and country styles. These examples of *kīrtan* performance are consonant with the plurality of accents, regions, centuries, religions, philosophical notes, classical rāgas, and folk tunes enshrined in the Guru Granth Sahib.

KARTARPUR

A question that remains for the future is whether there can be any moves toward rapprochement between Sikhs' historical heartland, the two Punjabs, severed since 1947 by the Pakistan-India border. For many decades only diaspora Sikhs have been able, relatively easily, to visit Sikh sacred sites in Pakistan such as Nankana Sahib and Panja Sahib. For Sikhs with Indian passports, however, it has been almost impossible. Of course, the digital world has brought opportunities for an online connectedness between Pakistanis and Indians.

Appropriately, in November 2019, Guru Nanak's 550th birth anniversary was marked by the inauguration of the Kartarpur corridor. This is a visa-free border crossing, via a new bridge, allowing Sikh pilgrims to travel from Dera Baba Nanak, near Gurdaspur in India, on the east bank of the river Ravi, to Gurdwara Darbar Sahib, at Kartarpur (near Narowal) on the west bank, the place where Guru Nanak spent the final years of his life and took his last breath in 1539.

The initiative was first proposed in 1999 by the prime ministers of India and Pakistan, and in 2018 the foundation stones were laid. Prime Minister Imran Khan of Pakistan declared that Pakistan was "not only opening the border but also their hearts for the Sikh community."

CONCLUSION

This chapter has suggested how the persistence of prejudice based on caste – and on gender – and inadequate understanding of the Guru Granth Sahib continue to be challenges. Moreover, major Sikh institutions need to be reformed. However, it is incontrovertible that nearly 500 years after his death, Guru Nanak is still a unifying force. The inclusiveness of the Gurus' emphasis on unicity, on *ikkoankār*, the oneness of all being, is in creative tension with those who would divide Muslims from Hindus and Sikhs, and it is interesting to see how it relates to assertions of Sikhs' separateness as a "nation." Any political ambition for the acknowledgment of Sikh nationhood needs to be grounded in the aspiration for a community – a *panth* and a Khalsa – in which all are one, whatever their gender, orientation, class, caste, or ethnicity.

As Sikhs embrace the latest technology and make significant contributions to national and global society, they draw inspiration from their history. In its complexity, Sikhs' at times traumatic history has the potential to foster and entrench divisive memories, but transcending these, the Gurus' spiritual insight is a resource for peaceful, purposeful coexistence. Sikhs' ever-evolving tradition of *sevā, sangat, langar*, and *kīrtan* is not only the strength of Sikhism but also a source of inspiration for all who encounter it.[22] Not only through its geographic spread but also through its global relevance, it has indeed proved itself to be a world religion.

NOTES

1 Anne Campbell Wilson, *After Five Years in India, or, Life and Work in a Punjaub District* (London: Blackie, 1895), 284.
2 Max Arthur Macauliffe, *The Sikh Religion: Its Gurus, Sacred Writings and Authors* (Oxford: Clarendon, 1909), lvii.
3 Macauliffe, *The Sikh Religion*, vi.
4 Khushwant Singh, *A History of the Sikhs Volume 2: 1839–1988*, 2nd ed. (New Delhi: Oxford University Press, 1999), 417.
5 Khushwant Singh, *A History of the Sikhs*, 416–417.
6 See Surinder S. Jodhka, "Sikh Idiom and the Making of the Punjabi Farmers' Movement of 2020–2021," in *The Indian Farmers' Protest of 2020–2021: Agrarian Crisis, Dissent and Ideology*, ed. Christine Moliner and David Singh (New Delhi: Routledge, 2024). See also Shinder S. Thandi, ed., *Farmer Resistance in Punjab: Mobilization and Resilience* (Abingdon: Routledge, 2023) and Navdeep Kaur, "Role of Memory in Farmers' Protest in India 2020–21; a Study," *Sikh Foundations Blog*, University of Michigan, 2022, https://sites.lsa.umich.edu/sikh-formations-podcast/2022/04/18/role-of-sikh-memory-in-farmers-protest-in-india-2020-21-a-study/.
7 Khushwant Singh, *A History of the Sikhs*, 305.
8 Dharam Singh, *Sikhism Today: Precepts and Perceptions* (Amritsar: Singh Brothers, 2023), 224–233.
9 See Eleanor Nesbitt, "Nanaksar," in *Brill's Encyclopedia of Sikhism, Vol. 1*, ed. Knut A. Jacobsen, Gurinder Singh Mann, Kristina Myrvold, and Eleanor Nesbitt (Leiden: Brill, **2017**, 380–385.
10 For detailed discussion of dietary principle and practice in the Sikh tradition, see Eleanor Nesbitt, "Vegetarianism," in *Brill's Encyclopedia of Sikhism, Vol. 2*, ed. Knut A. Jacobsen, Gurinder Singh Mann, Kristina Myrvold, and Eleanor Nesbitt (Leiden: Brill, 2025).
11 See Nikky-Guninder Kaur Singh, "Why Did I Not Light the Fire: The Refeminization of Ritual in Sikhism," *Journal of Feminist Studies in Religion* 16, no. 1 (2000): 63–85. For an alternative interpretation, see Pashaura Singh, *The Guru Granth Sahib: Canon, Meaning and Authority* (Oxford: Oxford University Press, 2000): 276–277.
12 Satwant Kaur Rait, *Sikh Women in England: Their Religious and Cultural Beliefs and Social Practices* (Stoke-on-Trent: Trentham Books, 2005), 55–94.
13 For a fuller discussion, see Nikky-Guninder Kaur Singh, *The Feminine Principle in the Sikh Vision of the Transcendent* (Cambridge: Cambridge University Press, 1993).
14 Jagir Jhutti Johal, *Sikhism Today* (London: A & C Black, 2011), 47–48.
15 Opinderjit Takhar, *Sikh Identity: An Exploration of Groups among Sikhs* (London: Routledge, 2005), 49–50.
16 See, for instance, Wendy Doniger and Brian Smith, trans., *The Laws of Manu* (Delhi: Penguin Classics, 1991).

17 Nikky-Guninder Kaur Singh, "Sikh Iconotexts for Global Society," in *The Bloomsbury Handbook of Religion, Gender, and Sexuality*, ed. Sonya Sharma, Dawn Llewellyn, and Sîan Hawthorne (London: Bloomsbury, 2024), 49–68.
18 Aleem Maqbool, "Jasvir Singh: 'I'm a Devout Sikh – and Married to a Man,'" BBC, February 4, 2023, https://www.bbc.co.uk/news/uk-64496456.
19 On Khalistan, see Shinder Thandi, "Emergent India and Its Sikh Diaspora," *India Forum: A Journal-Magazine on Contemporary Issues*, December 2023, theindiaforum.in/society/emergent-india-and-its-sikh-diaspora.
20 Gurminder Bhogal, "Tracking the Harmonium from Christian Missionary Hymns to Sikh Kirtan," *Yale Journal of Music & Religion* 8, no. 2 (2022): Article 1.
21 Neha Gohil, "First 'Globally Recognised' Music Exam for Sikh Sacred Music Launched in UK," *The Guardian*, **September 19, 2024.**
22 Simran Jeet Singh, *The Light We Give: How Sikh Wisdom Can Transform Your Life* (New York: Riverhead Books, 2022) exemplifies how Sikh insights can reach a wider public.

REFERENCES AND FURTHER READING

Moliner, Christine, and David Singh, eds. *The Indian Farmers' Protest of 2020–2021: Agrarian Crisis, Dissent and Ideology*. Delhi: Routledge, 2025.

Singh, Dharam. *Sikhism Today: Precepts and Perceptions*. Amritsar: Singh Brothers, 2023.

Singh, Gurharpal, and Giorgio Shani. *Sikh Nationalism: From a Dominant Minority to an Ethno-Religious Diaspora*. Cambridge: Cambridge University Press, 2021.

Singh, Simran Jeet. *The Light We Give: How Sikh Wisdom Can Transform Your Life*. New York: Riverhead Books, 2022.

Thandi, Shinder S., ed. *Farmer Resistance in Punjab: Mobilization and Resilience*. Abingdon: Routledge, 2023.

GLOSSARY

Akal(Akāl) Takht	Sikhs' seat of religious authority; building facing the Golden Temple
Akali	follower of the timeless One (Akāl), a warrior; also name of a Sikh political party
Akhanḍ pāṭh	uninterrupted reading of the entire Sikh scripture by a sequence of readers in 48 hours
amrit	"nectar of immortality"; empowered and empowering water used in initiation to Khalsa
Amritdhārī	Sikh who has been initiated by the *amrit* (nectar) ceremony.
anand kāraj	"rite of bliss," Sikh marriage ceremony
ardās	formal concluding prayer recited by a representative of the congregation with everybody standing up
Baisakhi	Sikh festival celebrating the spring harvest and the birth of the Khalsa
bāṇī	"speech"; divine word
beadabī	disrespect (particularly with reference to the Guru Granth Sāhib)
bhagat/bhakta	devotee; designation of saint-poets whose compositions are included in the Gurū Granth Sāhib
bhakti	love for the Divine
caste	endogamous group, associated with a particular occupation

DOI: 10.4324/9781003359210-8

Dalit	a person born into one of the most stigmatized castes
darshan	"seeing"; being in the presence of the Guru Granth
Dasam Granth	the book of the tenth Guru, created in his court
derā	religious establishment, typically under the control of a spiritual leader
dharam	morality, duty, religion
diaspora	community of people who live outside their homeland
divān	literally "court"; Sikh religious gathering
five Ks	The five items of faith worn on the Sikh body (*kesh, kanghā, kaṛā, kirpān*, and *kacchā*)
ghallūghārā	massacre, holocaust
granthī	reader of the Gurū Granth Sāhib, custodian of a gurdwara
gurdwara	Sikh place of worship
gurmatā	religious decision reached by authoritative Sikh assembly
gurmukh	Guru-centered, antithesis of self-centered *manmukh*s
Gurmukhi	sacred language of the Sikhs, the script for Punjabi language
Gurpurab	day commemorating the ten Gurus and historical events
Guru	medium of enlightenment
Guru Granth Sahib	the scriptural Guru, the epicenter of Sikh life
Harmandar Sahib	Golden Temple of modern times
haurmai	self-centered ego that splits the individual from the divine One
hukam	Divine design; passage from the Guru Granth Sahib opened at random and read as the message from the One
hukamnāmā	command; a reading from the Guru Granth Sahib after reverently opening it
Ikkoankār	the One Being
indentured laborer	laborer who is contracted to work for a specific number of years

janamsākhī	quasi-mythical narratives about the life of Guru Nanak
Japji	inaugural hymn of Sikh scripture by Guru Nanak in 38 stanzas recited daily by most Sikhs
Jāp	hymn by Guru Gobind Singh in 199 verses from the Dasam Granth
jathebandī	grouping of Sikhs, often united by respect for a particular religious leader
kacchā	long underpants, worn as one of the five Ks
kanghā	wooden comb, worn as one of the five Ks
kaṛā	steel/iron bracelet, worn as one of the five Ks
kaṛāh prashād	warm, sweet Sikh sacramental dish
karam	actions and the fruit of actions; karma
Kaur	"princess" (literally "prince"); surname for Sikh women
kesh	uncut hair, worn as one of the five Ks.
Khalistan	Land of the Pure, name of proposed Sikh independent state
Khalsa	"Pure," the new Sikh family birthed by the tenth Guru in 1699
khanḍā	double-edged sword; Sikh emblem comprising khanḍā, bisecting a circle and cupped by two kirpāns
kirpān	sword, worn as one of the five Ks
kīrtan	Sikh musical performance of divine praise
langar	Sikh communal meal, a desegregating commensality
lāvān	the bride and groom's circumambulation of the Guru Granth Sahib, the central element of *anand kāraj*
lekhā	Divine writing
manmukh	self-centered people, antithesis to the Guru-centered
maryādā	discipline
mīrī-pīrī	temporal (mīrī) and spiritual (pīrī) power
misl	18th-century group of armed Sikh horsemen with distinguishing title and battle standard
Mughal	Muslim rulers of much of India from the 16th to 18th century

mūl mantar	prelude to the Guru Granth Sahib, its central refrain, and keynote of Sikh prayers and ceremonies
nadar	look of divine love
nām simran	remembrance of the Divine in meditation
Nāmdhārī	follower of 19th-century reformer, Baba Ram Singh
Nirankārī	sect following Dayal Das and his successors
nishān sahib	Sikh flag. Serves as a marker for gurdwaras. It is saffron in color, triangular in shape, and is imprinted with the design of the *khanḍā*
panjābiat	Punjabi culture
pīrī	spiritual power
prakāsh	"bring to light," morning ceremony of opening the Guru Granth Sahib
qudrat	natural phenomena created by the Divine
rāga	musical mode
rāgi	Sikh musicians
rahit	code of Khalsa belief and conduct
rahitnāmā	manual listing Khalsa belief and conduct
sangat	Sikh religious gathering
sant	religious leader
Sarbat Khalsa	gathering of the whole (sarbat) Khalsa to make decisions
sarovar	pool of water, usually associated with a gurdwara
Sat nām	the true name
Sat Sri Akal	Sikh greeting, "Truth is the Timeless One"
Satguru	the true Guru
sevā	selfless service
SGPC	Shiromani Gurdwara Parbandhak Committee, elected committee that governs Sikh shrines
shabad	numinous word, also used for scriptural hymn
Sikh	student or disciple, name of the religious tradition

Singh	"Lion-hearted" (literally "lion"), surname for Sikh men
Singh Sabha	Sikh renaissance movement begun in 1873
Sufi	Muslim mystic
sukhāsan	"resting posture," evening ceremony of closing the Guru Granth Sahib
Waheguru	"Wondrous Guru," term for the divine One

INDEX

3HO 116, 162–3

Afghanistan 99–100, 106–7, 125
Africa 99, 101–2, 106, 111, 115–6
Akāl Takht 16, 25, 33–4, 44, 73, 75, 150, 153; see also *hukamnāmā* (2)
Akali (1) = Akali-Nihang 129, 161 (2); = political party 40, Akali Dal 151
Akhand Kirtani Jatha 41, 162
AKJ *see* Akhand Kirtani Jatha
alcohol 44, 159–60
Amar Das, Guru 12–14, 21, 76, 89
amrit 12 = *amrit* initiation 19, 23–4, 42, 76, 87–8, 115, 153
Amritsar 13–14, 25–31, 155–6, 159; Treaty of 33; *see also* Akāl Takht, Harmandar Sahib, Jallianwala Bagh
anand kāraj 13, 38, 88–9; mixed marriage 112; destination weddings 159
Anandpur 18–20, 75, 91
Anandpur Resolution 43–4
Angad, Guru 9–12, 21
Anglo-Sikh Wars 35, 43
ardās 16
Arjan, Guru 11, 14, 20–1, 26, 64–5, 85 and Guru Granth Sahib 15, 76–7, 80–1
art 3, 117, 121–32, 140–4
Australia 45, 100–1, 116–17, 162–3

Baisakhi 12–13; and Khalsa 19, 28, 31, 39, 44, 85–7; see also Jallianwala Bagh; Sant Nirankaris
Banda Singh see Singh, Banda
Bandi Chhoṛ Divas see Divālī
beadabī 159–60
beard see *kesh*
bhagat 2, 21; *see also* Singh, Puran Bhagat
bhangṛā 92
Bhatra (Bhat) 105
Bhindranwale, Jarnail Singh 44

calendar 84, 153–5; *see also* *gurpurab*, *melā*
Canada 45, 102–4, 109, 113–5, 138–9
caste 4, 14, 37, 93, 102, 141, 148, 150–2; rejected by Sikh teaching 19, 37, 42, 56. 62–3, 81–3; *see also* Bhatra, Jat, Ramgarhia, Ravidassia
Christian 36–37, 104, 108, 112, 133, 150–1
code of discipline *see rahit*

Dalit 150–2; *see also* Ravidassia
Dasam Granth 76, 125
death *see* funeral
derā 151–2
Dera Sach Khand Ballan 152

dharam 6, *28*, 63–7
diaspora 93, 96–117, 138–49, 142–4, 160–3
diet 41, 82, 153
Divālī 12, 30, 90–1, 154
dress 162; *see also* turban
drugs 44, 160
Duleep Singh *see* Singh, Duleep

environment 142, 153

Farmers' Movement (2020–2021) 113, 141–2, 148–9, 161
festival see *gurpurab, melā*
feticide *see* gender
film 96, 117–18, 139–40
First World War 36, 107
Five Beloved 19
Five Ks 36, 87, 153; *see also kanghā, kacchā; kaṛā, kesh; kirpān*
France 41, 107–8
funeral 89–90

gender 27–8, 134, 136–7, 139–40, 155–8
Germany 107
Gobind Singh, Guru 11, 18–21, 23–4, 28–9, 34, 43, 76, 78, 91, 134; as poet 124–7
Birthday 154
God 2, 6, 37, 42, 58–9, 158; *see also ikkoankār*, Waheguru
Golden Temple *see* Harmandar Sahib
greeting 28, 72
gurdwara 73–5, 81, 83, 87–9, 98, 101, 104, 110–12, 159; Guru Gobind Singh endowing 34; historic gurdwaras return to Sikh control 37, 40
Gurmukhi 3, 13–14, 21, 33, 37, 74, 114, 126–7, 143, 149; development 9, 11
gurpurab 44, 84–5
Guru 10; portraits of 124–5
Guru Granth Sahib 2, 6–7, 10, 13, 17, 20–4, 34, 38–9, 41–2, 72–5, 77, 84–8, 111, 114; see also *beadabī; hukamnāmā* (1)
Guru Nanak *see* Nanak, Guru
Guru Nanak Nishkam Sewak Jatha 115–16, 153

hair *see kesh*
Har Krishan, Guru 11, 17
Har Rai, Guru 11, 16–17
Hargobind, Guru 15–17, 124, 126
Harmandar Sahib 15, 32–4, 39, 46, 85–6, 90–1, 115, 127–9, 157–8
Hindu 2, 10, 15, 18, 28, 34, 38, 42, 49, 51, 73, 80, 83, 110, 134, 141, 148, 161
Hola Mohalla 91, 154
hukam 58–9
hukamnāmā = directive reading from Guru Granth Sahib, *vāk* (1) 26, 73; (2) = directive
from Akāl Takht 111, 159

ikkoankār 6, 48–51
Immigration Acts; Australia 101; Canada 103; New Zealand 101; UK 106; US 103
initiation see *amrit* initiation
Iraq 101, 117
Islam *see* Muslim
Italy 100, 107–8, 161

Jallianwala Bagh 39, 86, 137
janamsākhī 3–5, 80–81, 101, 123
Japji 7–8, 23, 48, 52, 56, 60, 58–70, 75–6, 79, 83
Jat 106, 150–1, 160

kacchā 20, 87
kanghā 20, 87
kaṛā 20, 87, 110
Kartarpur 8, 79, 143,163–4
Kaur 19, 139
Kenya *see* Africa
kesh 20, 42, 87, 96, 109, 162

Khalistan 45, 75, 104, 113, 160–1
Khalsa 18–20, 26, 85–87, 121, 126, 153; as a surname 116
khanḍ 65–70
khanḍā 19; as emblem 110–1
kirpān 109–10
kīrtan 8, 11, 79–80, 157, 162–3
Komagata Maru 103, 118

langar 8, 11–12, 29, 42, 46, 74, 80–2, 85–7, 90, 111–12, 116–17, 142, 146
language *see* Gurmukhi
literature 117, 132–9
Lohṛī 91, 156

Macauliffe, Max Arthur 39, 147–8
Malaysia 100, 114
Mani Singh *see* Singh, Mani
marriage *see anand kāraj*
martial arts 114, 161
martyr *see shahīd*
melā see Baisakhi; Divālī; Hola Mohalla; Lohṛī
mukti 64, 69
mūl mantar, 33, 48–50, 57–8, 69, 87, 122
music 2; *see also kīrtan*, rāga
Muslim 3–4, 10, 15, 18, 21, 34, 80, 117, 126–7, 132, 134–6, 144, 153, 158
Myanmar 38, 100, 111

Nabha, Kahn Singh 38–40
Namdhari 31–6, 37–8, 41, 109
name giving 86–7, 156
Nanak, Guru 2–5, 9, 55, 60–70, 79, 82, 164 poet 6–8, 10, 21, 76; *see also janamsākhī*
Nanaksar 41, 115
Nanded 20, 34, 75, 126
New Zealand 101
Nihang *see* Akali-Nihang
Nirankari 37–8; *see also* Sant Nirankari
nisān/nishān 16, 110, 122, 149
nitnem see prayer
North America see Canada, United States

Pakistan 34, 41–2, 34, 99, 143–14. 153–5, 163–4
Panj Piare *see* Five Beloved
persecution *see shahīd*
philanthropy 14, 84, 93, 115
prayer 54, 75–7; *see also* ardās
Pritam, Amrita 135–7
Punjab 2, 43, 115, 126, 130–3, 148–51, 154–5,163; number of Sikhs 27; and Maharaja

Ranjit Singh 32, 35; Partition 41
rāga 22
rahit 144, 153
Rahit Maryādā *see* Sikh Rahit Maryādā
rahitnāmā 27, 40, 125
Ram Das, Guru 11, 13–14, 21, 42, 76
Ramgarhia 102, 105–6, 115, 131
Ranjit Singh, maharaja 25, 32–35, 122; patron of arts 126–9
Ravidassia 23, 106, 152, 159
rite of passage *see amrit*-initiation; *anand kāraj*; funeral; name-giving

sac 51–2, 65, 69–70
sangat 8, 77–9, 150
sant 115–16, 152–3
Sant Nirankari 44
schools 109, 110, 114
Second World War 41, 101
sevā 1, 42, 45–6, 82–4, 116–17, 149, 153
sexuality 158–9
shahīd 85, 137
Shiromani Gurdwara Parbandhak Committee see SGPC
SGPC 40, 112, 117, 150–1, 153
Sikh Rahit Maryādā 26, 40–2, 88, 125, 159

Sikh Studies 114–5
Singapore 99, 103, 114
Singh 19, 87
Singh, Banda 28–9
Singh, Duleep 35, 105, 107; film 117–18
Singh, Khushwant 45, 136, 140, 148–9
Singh, Mani 28–31
Singh, Puran (Bhagat) 45–6
sport 113–14; *see also* martial arts
Sundari, Mata 20, 28–9

takht 34, 75; *see also* Akāl Takht, Nanded
Tanzania *see* Africa
Tegh Bahadar, Guru 11, 17–18, 21, 23, 141
Thailand 100–101, 114
turban 96, 124, 156; disputes 100, 108–9, 116; turban day 108; women wearing 41, 116, 153, 162

Uganda *see* Africa
United Kingdom 45–6, 81, 89, 102, 104–6, 109–18, 139–40, 153, 158, 160–2
United States 45, 96, 102–4, 109–10, 112, 114–5, 139, 143

Vaisakhi *see* Baisakhi
vāk see hukamnāmā (1)
vegetarianism *see* diet

Waheguru 2, 28, 41, 72, 77, 150, 158
women *see* gender

www.ingramcontent.com/pod-product-compliance
Ingram Content Group Australia Pty Ltd
76 Discovery Rd, Dandenong South VIC 3175, AU
AUHW011525090726
429692AU00011B/92

9 781032 416779